Cambri

Elements in the Global Middle Ages
edited by
Geraldine Heng
University of Texas at Austin
Susan Noakes
University of Minnesota Twin Cities

OCEANIA, 800–1800CE

A Millennium of Interactions in a Sea of Islands

James L. Flexner
University of Sydney

CAMBRIDGE
UNIVERSITY PRESS

CAMBRIDGE
UNIVERSITY PRESS

University Printing House, Cambridge CB2 8BS, United Kingdom

One Liberty Plaza, 20th Floor, New York, NY 10006, USA

477 Williamstown Road, Port Melbourne, VIC 3207, Australia

314–321, 3rd Floor, Plot 3, Splendor Forum, Jasola District Centre,
New Delhi – 110025, India

103 Penang Road, #05–06/07, Visioncrest Commercial, Singapore 238467

Cambridge University Press is part of the University of Cambridge.

It furthers the University's mission by disseminating knowledge in the pursuit of
education, learning, and research at the highest international levels of excellence.

www.cambridge.org
Information on this title: www.cambridge.org/9781108823289
DOI: 10.1017/9781108913782

First published 2021

A catalogue record for this publication is available from the British Library.

ISBN 978-1-108-82328-9 Paperback
ISSN 2632-3427 (online)
ISSN 2632-3419 (print)

Oceania, 800–1800CE

A Millennium of Interactions in a Sea of Islands

Elements in the Global Middle Ages

DOI: 10.1017/9781108913782
First published online: November 2021

James L. Flexner
University of Sydney
Author for correspondence: James L. Flexner, James.flexner@sydney.edu.au

Abstract: Over a span of 1,000 years beginning around 800CE, the people of the Pacific Islands undertook a remarkable period of voyaging, political evolution, and cross-cultural interactions. Polynesian navigators encountered previously uninhabited lands, as well as already inhabited islands and the coast of the Americas. Island societies saw epic sagas of political competition and intrigue, documented through oral traditions and the monuments and artefacts recovered through archaeology. European entry into the region added a new episode of interaction with strange people from over the horizon. These histories provide an important cross-cultural perspective for the concept of 'the Middle Ages' from outside of the usual Old World focus.

Keywords: Oceania, Global Middle Ages, cross-cultural interaction, Pacific history, Pacific archaeology

ISBNs: 9781108823289 (PB), 9781108913782 (OC)
ISSNs: 2632-3427 (online), 2632-3419 (print)

Contents

1 Oceania's Island World: Geographic and Conceptual Background

Oceania, comprising thousands of islands scattered across the Pacific Ocean, covers roughly one third of the Earth's surface. Many of the islands are quite small, spread across an area completely dominated by the sea. Oceania sits outside of the normal geographical scope of studies of the 'Middle Ages', which is a phenomenon generally assumed to apply to Europe, and sometimes more generously including parts of Africa or Asia. The Americas, Australia, and the Pacific are consistently thought to be outside of this topic of study (though see also Bairnes' forthcoming work in this series).

Such a definition is reasonable if the Middle Ages or Medieval period are thought of as primarily a European historical time period or cultural phenomenon with echoes in neighbouring regions. If, however, the Middle Ages are thought of in terms of their thematic content, then the narrative shifts quite considerably. The Middle Ages are no longer considered a 'Dark Age' of societal collapse and turmoil following the dissolution of the Roman Empire. Increasingly, scholars point to a historical era of new opportunities for the movement of people, things, and ideas, and a flourishing of new forms of cultural, religious, political, and creative expression. If that is the case, then Oceania certainly fits thematically within the latter definition (see also Williams 2021, which was published while this Element was in press). This Element focuses on the Oceanic region between 800CE, after which Polynesian navigators embarked on a major period of navigation and expansion, and the period of initial European encounters in the region, which ends roughly 1,000 years later.

The goal of this Element is not at all a specialist's gripe about how my area of interest has been neglected by scholars working in other regions. Quite the opposite: given the breadth and richness of studies in the Global Middle Ages, as expressed in this series and other works (e.g., Holmes and Standen 2018), Oceania simply provides another example of a broader process of cultural fluorescence and evolution during the period falling in and around the Middle Ages. There is already some productive comparative work being done for Oceania during this time period, for example examining the parallel and divergent trajectories of Viking-age Scandinavian societies with the ancient Hawaiian kingdoms (Price 2018; Price and Ljunkgvist 2018; Ravn 2018). Hopefully this Element will encourage Middle Ages specialists to look more broadly across the Pacific region, without falling into the trap of overly-simplistic analogising (Spriggs 2008, 2016).

The Element is also not a complete synthesis of Pacific archaeology or history (see instead Leclerc and Flexner 2019; Kirch 2017; Kirch and Green 2001;

Rainbird 2004; Spriggs 1997). It is not possible to cover every archipelago and period to the same depth, and I have not sought to do so. Instead, this study offers broad coverage across Oceania while also developing the stories from the islands with which I am most familiar in Hawai'i, Aotearoa (New Zealand), and Vanuatu. This Element seeks to introduce the reader to the reasons Oceania would be of interest in relation to the Global Middle Ages, using a series of illustrative examples. For those looking for a deeper dive into Pacific history and prehistory, I offer extensive references for further reading.

This Element is primarily archaeological in its outlook, though it also draws on anthropological and historical research to construct its narrative. The European Middle Ages are often defined temporally as having taken place during the millennium preceding 1492. Because of the history of voyaging, settlement, and interaction in Oceania, the narrative here begins slightly later, during the century when Polynesian people left the ancestral homelands of Tonga and Samoa and began sailing towards the east after about 800CE (Kirch 2017: 191–208). The study ends a millennium later during a period when the region was initially drawn into the globalising world system (*sensu* Wallerstein 1974) expanding from early modern Europe as the Middle Ages came to an end. The goal is to write a history that extends to some extent across the 'prehistory/history divide' (Lightfoot 1995), in order to show the creative ways in which Pacific Islanders adapted to colonial encounters during the early years of their interactions with Europeans. These engagements would set the scene for the more intensive period of European colonialism that began after 1800CE, which falls beyond the scope of this series (see instead Flexner 2014a, 2020; Lydon 2006; Smith 2014).

Initial settlement of the Pacific region included colonisation of uninhabited lands by maritime navigators, beginning with some of the first islands colonised after behaviourally modern *Homo sapiens* left Africa during the Pleistocene (the last Ice Age), including the earliest known sea voyages (see Kealy et al. 2016). New Guinea has been inhabited for at least 40,000 years, including Pleistocene occupation of the mountainous interior (Gosden 2010; Fairbairn et al. 2017). If some of the earliest dates from northern Australia are reliable, initial human colonisation of the region could be pushed back closer to 60,000–70,000 years (Clarkson et al. 2017). While beyond the scope of this Element to discuss in detail, it should be noted that New Guinea was also an independent centre of early plant domestication and cultivation, including the key Oceanic crops of yams, taro, bananas, and sugarcane (Golson et al. 2017).

This longer-term history is important for understanding some of the variability and diversity of Oceanic societies and their more recent pasts. The pre-eminent Pacific archaeologist Roger Green (1991) proposed that the region could be divided into 'Near Oceania', those areas first settled during the Pleistocene encompassing the islands of New Guinea and the Solomon Islands as far south as Makira, and 'Remote Oceania', the area of the Pacific first settled by the people of the Lapita Cultural Complex and their descendants (Kirch 1997b). Near Oceania, and the region referred to as Island Melanesia more generally, sees the greatest concentrations of cultural, biological, and linguistic diversity in the Pacific (Spriggs 1997). People in Near Oceania speak both Austronesian languages, generally agreed to have developed from ancestral forms in Island Southeast Asia with further creolisation and evolution across the Pacific, and Non-Austronesian or 'Papuan' languages, thought to have originated from Near Oceania's preliminary settlers during the last Ice Age which likewise would have transformed, diversified, and proliferated over time.

The part of Remote Oceania known as Polynesia, settled later and by smaller, more uniform founding populations, has more closely related cultures that arguably hold together as a 'phyletic unit', having evolved from a common ancestral society that can be reconstructed on linguistic, anthropological, and archaeological grounds (Kirch and Green 2001; see below for a discussion of the problematic nature of the Melanesia/Polynesia divide). It was the Polynesian navigators who reached the last of the islands in Oceania to be initially settled beginning around 900 years ago.

Finally, it should be noted that while our understanding of Pacific archaeology has advanced by leaps and bounds over the past two decades, particularly for the period commonly called 'prehistory', knowledge in the region remains markedly uneven. Large areas remain unsurveyed by archaeologists and many time periods remain poorly represented, particularly in Island Melanesia (see discussion in Kirch 2017: 9–10). In New Zealand initial settlement has been dated to within a generation around roughly 1250CE using high-precision calibrated radiocarbon dates. This date matches the genealogical estimates for the timing of first settlement based on Māori historical traditions (see Wilmshurst et al. 2011: 1817). Even more remarkably in Tonga the initial date of Lapita settlement has been narrowed to a span of a few years (2838±8 years before present) thanks to the super-precise technique of coral dating using uranium and thorium isotopes (Burley et al. 2012). Contrast this with places like the central Solomon Islands (Walter and Sheppard 2017) or southern Vanuatu (Flexner et al. 2018a) where, while work is ongoing, we are only beginning to construct a reasonable picture of basic culture history. Rather than despairing, though, this should be seen as an encouragement to any intrepid students interested in working in a fascinating area of the world with incredible people and much to learn!

2 Timeless Backwater, or Written Out of History?

When Europeans began defining the culture areas of the world they had conquered over the course of the 1700s and 1800s, the peoples of Oceania were generally classified as 'Neolithic'. They made ground-stone tools, practised agriculture, and in some cases, though not all, produced pottery. As such, they were placed on an imaginary and misleading evolutionary ladder that located the 'hunter-gatherer' populations of, for example, Aboriginal Australia towards the bottom. The people of Oceania sat higher on the ladder but below, for example, metal-producing societies in Africa and Asia. European 'civilisations', particularly the great empires of Britain or France, represented the pinnacle of human achievement. In reflecting on the definition of stone tools collected from living people as 'archaeological' in the Pitt Rivers Museum, Hicks (2013: 4) refers to this as 'the anthropological trick of collapsing geographical distance into temporal distance'. In other words, classifying living peoples as 'contemporary ancestors' or 'survivals', holdouts from earlier periods in history from which Europe had long since progressed, was a convenient myth for justifying European conquest and colonialism (Fabian 1983).

The absurdity of this exercise can be demonstrated through the arbitrary choice of technology used in the ranking system. The standard European classification had humanity progressing through ages of stone, bronze, iron, and onward into protohistoric and historical civilisations, ending with the great colonial empires of the nineteenth century. But if another trait and moment in time is used as the focus, say, sailing technology in the 1400s, a different picture appears. While the Portuguese were still struggling to reliably cross the equatorial doldrums, the Swahili maritime world was emerging along the coast of eastern Africa (Fleisher et al. 2015; Kusimba forthcoming). The Chinese built huge ships not for deep-water voyaging but rather to carry massive amounts of people and cargo closer to shore, participating in Indian Ocean trade including with the Swahili (Pomeranz 2009: 72–3). At the same time Oceanic master navigators were regularly and reliably making return voyages of thousands of kilometers on their *waka* (double-hulled sailing canoes; see Doran 1981; Haddon and Hornell 1938).

The pre-eminent Pacific scholar Epeli Hau'ofa (1993) defined Oceania as a 'sea of islands' (Figure 1). For Islanders, the ocean represented not a boundary or obstacle, but a fluid medium for long-distance interactions and a bountiful resource, perhaps more so than for people from any other part of the world. However, the point here is not to choose another measure to show that Polynesians were somehow 'better' or more advanced than Europeans or

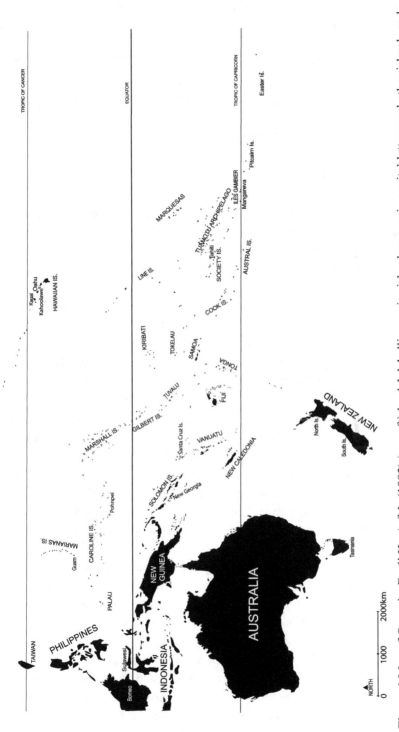

Figure 1 Map of Oceania, Epeli Hau'ofa's (1993) 'sea of islands', labelling major island groups in capital letters and other islands and locations mentioned in the text. Note I was not able to label every single island mentioned in the text at this scale, but more detailed maps are available in the referenced publications.

anyone else. The aim is to demonstrate that this kind of 'progress'-oriented colonial perspective on human achievement needs to be challenged and rejected as it is unhelpful for understanding global histories.

Decades of scholarship from anthropologists, historians, and others has refuted and overturned the Eurocentric mythology that attempts to rank human societies as more or less 'evolved'. In many cases the 'primitive' peoples whose societies were documented and classified by colonial anthropology, including those in Oceania, were dramatically transformed by the upheavals of colonial encounter and empire (Wolf 1982; see also Sand 2002; Sand et al. 2003; Spriggs 2008). Among other things, a better understanding of how social evolution actually works demonstrates that such a ranking system is not justified scientifically or logically. Rather, evolutionary anthropology can outline the ways that related cultures have changed through time while also acknowledging that all social forms have their own versions of complexity (for Pacific examples of evolutionary anthropological scholarship see Cochrane 2021; Kirch 2021; Kirch and Green 2001).

Despite apparent progress in anthropological thought, broader popular narratives about the Pacific often reproduce precisely the kinds of colonialist ideological constructs described above. There are of course the obvious tropes of simple, smiling islanders living in tropical paradise, or, worse, bloodthirsty cannibal feasts in the dark jungles, both of which can be rejected as inappropriate and indeed hurtful for living Pacific Islanders. But there are also more subtle forms of colonial thinking that are worth challenging. For example, Diamond's (2005) use of Rapa Nui (Easter Island) as one of the major case studies in his writing about the 'collapse' of past societies has proven a compelling popular science narrative. As will be seen below this narrative misses some of the key evidence for the actual processes through which Rapa Nui's landscape was transformed by human activity (see Hunt and Lipo 2009). Here as elsewhere in the Pacific, European colonial activities prove to be a major culprit for the island's apparent environmental degradation.

One of the major historical works that continues to shape perceptions of different areas of the Pacific is Dumont D'Urville's 'Sur les îles du Grand Océan', published in the *Bulletin de la Société de Géographie* in 1832 (see Clark 2003). D'Urville proposed three sub-regions in the Pacific: Polynesia, Melanesia, and Micronesia (see Figure 2). Polynesia ('many islands') consisted of the great triangle with Hawai'i, Rapa Nui, and Aotearoa (New Zealand) at the corners, plus the western 'homeland' of Samoa and Tonga. Micronesia ('tiny islands') was defined by its geographical features as consisting primarily of small islands and atolls, including some inhabited islands only a few kilometres in surface area with high points just a few meters above sea level. Finally, and

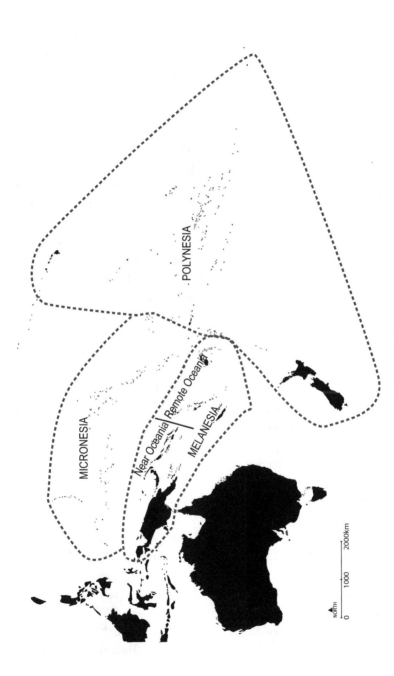

Figure 2 Oceania showing the boundaries of Polynesia, Micronesia, and Melanesia, along with Green's (1991) alternative division between Near and Remote Oceania.

most problematically, Melanesia ('dark islands') was defined by the 'racial' characteristics of the islands' inhabitants, who had dark skin and 'wooly' hair. Following the logic of the time, Dumont D'Urville and subsequent anthropological scholars placed the lighter-skinned Polynesians above the darker inhabitants of Melanesia, while Micronesians sat somewhere in between as their social organisation and material culture was believed to be 'simpler' than that of the Polynesians.

The twentieth-century extension of this logic saw a distinction created between the more complex hierarchical and hereditary 'chiefdoms' of Polynesia, and the 'simpler' peoples of Melanesia who had ranked societies of 'big men' who achieved their position but did not have the level of sophistication reached on the other side of the Polynesia/Melanesia divide (see discussion in Sahlins 1963). This classification made two major errors. First, it masked the immense diversity within each of these regions. Melanesia holds most of the diversity of human cultures and languages in Oceania. Just the small island nation of Vanuatu, with eighty-five inhabited islands and a current population approaching 280,000, is home to around 100 distinct languages (Crowley 2000). The Solomon Islands and Papua New Guinea exhibit similar diversity (Greenhill 2015; Pawley 2009). Significantly, these areas include languages from the Polynesian family, evidence of an imaginary colonial boundary that was in fact permeable, something to be covered below in the section on the history of Polynesian Outliers.

Second, the apparent simplicity of the Melanesian societies as documented by colonial anthropologists is an artefact of intentional and unintentional bias, as well as the social, ecological, economic, and demographic disruptions that resulted from encounter and entanglement with European empires from the 1500s to the 1900s (see Spriggs 2008). The apparent difference across the Polynesia/Melanesia divide has shaped to some degree the history of archaeological scholarship in the Pacific. Melanesian archaeology focused on early, pottery-bearing sites, while archaeology on the other side of the boundary emphasised the large stone constructions of Polynesian chiefs and their followers (see Kirch 2017: 13–32). Archaeological research since the 1980s has shown that Melanesians in fact also lived in large aggregated settlements, built complex stone structures both in the form of agricultural terraces and ritual constructions, and exhibited a high degree of socio-political complexity. This has been demonstrated clearly for New Caledonia (Sand 1996, 2002), the Solomon Islands (Walter et al. 2004), and Vanuatu (Bedford 2019; Spriggs 1981, 1986).

Again the point is not to show that Melanesians have somehow reached the same 'stage' or level of complexity as the Polynesians. Rather, this perspective undermines the very divisions that Dumont D'Urville originally proposed, even as we still use them as a geographic heuristic in contemporary scholarship (Flexner and Leclerc 2019). Not only does the entire Oceanic region have a rich and complex history, but this history is significant and informative for comparative perspectives in other parts of the world, including for topics such as 'the Middle Ages'.

In the remaining pages of this Element, I focus on the concept of interactions for an Oceanic world over a period covering roughly 1,000 years. This begins with some of the last human colonisations of undiscovered lands, 'pristine' islands including the ones at the vertices of the great Polynesian triangle: Hawai'i, Rapa Nui (Easter Island), and Aotearoa (New Zealand). These encounters represent important examples of the kinds of environmental learning that people had to undertake to figure out how to survive in ecosystems that pushed the limits of their transported agricultural systems. Voyages to the east brought Polynesians into encounters with the Pacific coastal peoples of South America, and possibly North America (though the latter is a more controversial claim; see Jones and Klar 2012). In the other direction, voyages to the west brought Polynesians back into contact with populations with whom they shared a common ancestry, resulting in the formation of 'Polynesian Outliers'.

Far from being nomadic sailors, Oceanic peoples lived on islands over many generations, establishing lineages, political rivalries, and mythic historicities (see Ballard 2014). With the possible exception of the enigmatic *rongorongo* script of Rapa Nui, likely a protohistoric invention resulting from Spanish contacts in the 1700s (Fischer 1997), Pacific Islanders did not record their stories in writing. Thus much of what we know about social and political history in Oceania prior to European contacts comes from oral traditions, many of which were written down beginning in the nineteenth century, by European explorers, missionaries, and anthropologists (e.g., Fornander 1917; Gray 1892, 1894; Humphreys 1926), and in some cases by Native scholars such as Kamuela Kamakau and Davida Malo in Hawai'i (Kamakau 1976, 1991; Malo 1951). For much of the 19th and 20th centuries much of the content of these traditions was treated as mythical in nature: stories that structured cultural beliefs and identities to maintain cohesion and stability in small island societies. Increasingly by the last decades of the twentieth century, scholars determined that these stories recorded actual histories (see Dye 1989; Garanger 1996; Kirch 2010a). The names of the individuals and the feats involved really did happen. Even where the stories are augmented with magical events or supernatural explanations for happenings, there is an underlying element of factuality. These traditions allow for alternative interpretations of the material record of archaeological evidence (David et al. 2012; Flexner 2014b; Kirch 2018). Archaeological research has subsequently added richness and depth to our understanding of past dynamics in these complex island societies (Kirch 2017).

One of the points of this Element is to treat European expansion into Oceania not as a distinct break with the indigenous past, but part of a longer history of interactions and incursions by various newcomers over shorter and longer periods. At the same time, it has to be acknowledged that the presence of Europeans did cause major upheaval among island societies, not least because of the significant demographic decline caused by introduced diseases. Thus I do provide a separate section on European colonial encounters and invasions. During a period covering almost 300 years, different groups of Oceanic people had initial interactions with explorers and sailors beginning with Magellan in 1519 and basically finishing with Cook, whose great voyages in the Southern Ocean ended in 1779. Poignantly, both of these voyages that bookend the 'heroic' era of European exploration in the Pacific end with the deaths of the now famous navigators at the hands of Islanders.

Major incursions by the European powers and attempts to dominate or even exterminate Oceanic populations did not begin until well into the 1800s. In some cases Europeans, their things, and their ideas were barely present for Islander societies even into the twentieth century, as was the case in the New Guinea Highlands, for example (see Gosden 2004: 93–103). There is a long period of early European 'contacts' that pre-dates the major upheavals in Oceanic societies beginning in the nineteenth century (Flexner 2014a) that is nonetheless relevant to the broader narrative here for what it shows about the adaptability and resilience of Pacific Islanders in their ability to accommodate and respond to outside influences.

Finally, the Element closes with a discussion of what the Pacific past means for the future of Islander societies. People in the region face a number of challenges as the twenty-first century enters its third decade, from climate change, to conflicts over resources, to the struggles faced by some of the world's youngest democratic nation-states. However, I will present an argument that the knowledge produced by centuries of scholarship encapsulating the wisdom of Oceanic peoples, including increasingly the scholarship led by indigenous Islanders, is cause for some optimism regarding the ways that Pacific Island societies might continue to adapt during the next 1,000 years of their history.

3 Encountering New Environments: The Ends of Polynesia

The settlement of the Polynesian islands is one of the great epics of human exploration, discovery, and settlement (Kirch 2010b). As the New Zealand Māori scholar Ranginui Walker (1990: 24) framed the story, 'Within a time frame of 600 years Polynesians had colonised an oceanic environment that was 995 parts water to five parts land. Given the period in human history when this task was accomplished . . . it was a remarkable achievement.' This accomplishment has been made even more remarkable through the emerging evidence that this period of exploration was likely even shorter than Walker estimated. The exact timing and nature of initial settlement remains a matter of vibrant debate among Pacific archaeologists. Horsburgh and McCoy (2017) provide a current synthesis of the state of this discussion. Much of the argument about chronology is highly technical in nature, revolving around the visibility of evidence for initial settlement, the reliability of different kinds of radiocarbon dates, and statistical methods (see Dye 2015; Mulrooney et al. 2011; Wilmshurst et al. 2011).

While this story will doubtless be refined as better evidence is found and methods are improved, a general picture has emerged over the last twenty years or so. Before 900CE, Polynesian people began voyaging eastward beyond the 'homeland' of Tonga and Samoa. One thing that is clear from various forms of evidence is that the subsequent discovery and settlement of every inhabitable island in the Pacific must have been intentional and systematic. Computer models developed since the 1970s have shown that for many of the islands in the Pacific, accidental discovery would be impossible because of the nature of wind, ocean currents, and geography in the region (e.g., Irwin 1992; Levison et al. 1972). Then there were the oral traditions of the Islanders themselves, many of which record specific voyages by named individuals, often involving return trips covering thousands of kilometres (Howe 2006; see below). Greater understanding of Polynesian navigation has also been gained through modern experimental voyaging undertaken since the 1970s on ships such as *Hokule'a* (Finney 1979). This traditional Polynesian double-hulled sailing canoe has now sailed not only to destinations around the Pacific but has gone on to circumnavigate the globe using traditional navigation techniques.

Long-distance voyaging in Polynesia was largely carried out using double-hulled canoes, though there were also canoes with a larger main hull and an outrigger for stability. The double-hulled examples included a superstructure containing a house for the sailors that kept dry the plants, cooking fire, and other articles that were key to the long voyages. Sails were of a variety of forms, from triangular to 'crab claw'-shaped, and usually made of fine woven mats. The rigging was designed to be put up and taken down quickly, and could be easily pivoted depending on the direction of the wind. There is very little primary archaeological evidence for what traditional voyaging canoes looked like, since the organic materials from which they were constructed do not preserve well in Oceania's humid tropical environments. Most of what is known about these remarkable vessels is derived from early European explorers' accounts, linguistic evidence, and ethnography (e.g., Doran 1981; Haddon and Hornell 1938).

There are a few notable examples of direct archaeological evidence for Polynesian seagoing vessels. At Vaito 'otia-Fa'ahia, a waterlogged site from Huahine in the Society Islands excavated by Yoshihiko Sinoto in the 1970s that dates to between the 1200s and 1500s CE, there are multiple preserved timber beams measuring up to 7 m in length. The beams were almost certainly part of a canoe hull, and include lashing holes that hint at past construction techniques. They were recovered alongside a steering paddle of at least 4 m in length (Sinoto 1979; Sinoto and McCoy 1975). A more complete portion of canoe hull dating to roughly 1400CE was recovered more recently in Anaweka, Aotearoa (New Zealand). The hull is also from a canoe constructed of sewn and caulked planks. It features a carved sea turtle on what might have been the prow of the vessel, assuming the turtle was meant to point in the direction of travel. The turtle is an important symbol of voyaging since turtles were and are known to circumscribe routes of thousands of kilometers in the Pacific Ocean, as well as possibly representing connection to ancestral tropical Polynesia. Reconstruction of the canoe suggests a double-hulled vessel that would have measured up to 20 m in length and would have been suitable for deep-sea voyaging (Johns et al. 2014).

Heyerdahl's (1952) hypothesis of a South American origin for Polynesians, which he set out to prove during the infamous 'Kon Tiki' voyages (Melander 2019), did not stand the test of time. Archaeologists now universally accept that the Polynesians must have sailed systematically from west to east in search of new lands, though, as will be discussed below, they did reach the Pacific coast of the Americas from this direction. However, this does not mean that tales of South American drift voyaging have disappeared completely, as geneticists recently revived the hypothesis on the basis of evidence for Native American DNA in modern Marquesan populations (Ioannidis et al. 2020). Given the distance involved (over 7,000 km to Ecuador, which is identified as the most likely origin place) and the vagaries of genetic 'dating' as a technique, a more parsimonious explanation is that the genetic exchange happened much more recently during the period of Spanish colonialism. There remains the alternative possibility that the genetic evidence shows that some South Americans chose to sail with their Polynesian visitors during that contact event (see below).

Most evidence for Polynesian settlement converges on a burst of voyaging and discovery around the period of 900–1100CE (see Kirch 2017: 198–201). During this period people had settled into the Cook Islands, Marquesas, Tahiti, and the surrounding areas of Central Polynesia. The number of sites relating to this period of initial colonisation is fleetingly small, and in many cases it is difficult to argue that an early site is definitively 'the' arrival point for the first canoes to reach a certain island. However, advances in radiocarbon and other isotopic dating methods have allowed archaeologists to begin accumulating the data to better understand the nature of exploration and settlement in Oceania. Evidence from 'Kitchen Cave' on the island of Kamaka in the Mangareva group has revealed the earliest known human presence in the form of a coral abrader that was dated to 860±5 CE. This is several centuries earlier than the primary evidence for large-scale human occupation in the form of radiocarbon dates from the 1100s–1300s CE. The gap suggests that at least in this case Polynesian navigators were aware of the location of a group of islands for several centuries before a concerted effort to settle took place (Kirch et al. 2021). Considering the limited agricultural potential in Mangareva (Conte and Kirch 2004; Kirch et al. 2015), perhaps it is not a surprise that it was not immediately attractive for permanent settlement.

Recent research using microscopic evidence from sediment cores likewise suggests an early period of incremental systematic voyaging during which Polynesian explorers gathered new knowledge of islands in Central and Eastern Polynesia that coincided with a period of serious drought to the west. Microscopic 'biomarkers' relating to the activities of humans and their commensal animals, particularly pigs, were found in lake sediment cores from the island of Atiu in the Cook Islands. The biomarkers revealed early human presence by about 900CE, roughly two centuries earlier than the evidence for major landscape disturbance associated with large-scale settlement. Comparison with other lake sediments from Vanuatu and Samoa, along with published palaeoclimate data from other islands, indicated a period of relatively dry weather. Wetter conditions returned beginning around 1150CE, which coincides with the next period of great discoveries in Polynesia (Sear et al. 2020). The subsequent pulse of navigation established human populations on the vertices of Polynesia's great triangle (Horsburgh and McCoy 2017: 6–8). Hawai'i was definitely settled by the 1200s (Rieth et al. 2011), and likely a bit earlier than that (Athens et al. 2014 estimate 1000–1100CE); Aotearoa (New Zealand) was settled around 1250CE (Jacomb et al. 2014), while Rapa Nui (Easter Island) was probably first settled somewhere in between, during the 1200s (Hunt and Lipo 2009).

This is not to say that environment completely determined the nature of Polynesian exploration. The motivation for people to load their families, crops, and household objects onto double-hulled canoes in search of new islands was driven by a combination of environmental conditions, cultural beliefs, and social dynamics, all of which fed into each other. Kirch (2017: 270–1) has suggested that one social cause lies in the kinship structure of

Polynesian chiefly systems. Inheritance was strongly linked to primogeniture, such that a first-born son of a high-ranking chief would expect the lion's share of family lands, titles, and property. Subsequent chiefly sons' ambitions would lie over the horizon. Polynesian societies also placed great honour and value on those who were capable of making successful voyages. These were exploring societies, and people who discovered new islands and returned home to tell the tale doubtless enhanced their *mana* (spiritual power or prestige).

Some of the great navigators of this era have had their names and deeds passed down through history. *Moʻolelo*, Hawaiian traditions, about these epic journeys are particularly rich, having been written down from their original sources during the nineteenth century. The stories reflect deep cultural truths about chiefly rivalries, resource stresses, and political motivations for long-distance voyaging. One example is the story of Pāʻao, who was the younger brother of the chief Lonopele. The two lived on the same island in Tahiti and often quarrelled over land and resources. Pāʻao was a powerful priest, and owner of the war god Kū kā ʻili moku. Lonopele tricked Pāʻao into killing his own son. Pāʻao in his grief prepared to sail away, and during the period where his canoe was *kapu* (taboo) he sacrificed Lonopele's son in turn, simultaneously fulfilling a sacred responsibility and securing his exile. Eventually Pāʻao landed in Hawaiʻi, where he was said to have introduced the cult of Kū, including the practice of human sacrifice, establishing important priestly lineages and leading the construction of several prominent temples (Kamakau 1991: 3–5; Kirch 2010a: 86).

ʻOlopana and Moʻikeha were another pair of younger brothers from Hawaiʻi Island who saw their prospects dwindle as elder siblings gained the best lands and fishing grounds. They plotted to attack their brother Kumuhonua but were fought off. Their lives were spared, but they were exiled. After a flood destroyed their home in Waipiʻo Valley (Figure 3), the brothers decided to sail to their ancestral homeland in ʻKahikiʼ (Tahiti) with their retainers. ʻOlopana decided to stay in Tahiti but Moʻikeha returned home, visiting each of the Hawaiian Islands before being welcomed in Kauaʻi, where he settled. Late in life Moʻikeha desired to see his son Laʻa, who had been left behind as an infant in Tahiti. A canoe was sent to gather Laʻa, also called Laʻa-mai-Kahiki (Laʻa from Tahiti), who visited his father for some time before returning home (Fornander 1917: 113–25; Kirch 2010a: 85–6). The voyages of Pāʻao, Moʻikeha, and the other great voyagers of this era likely took place during the 1300s CE, after which the *moʻolelo* cease recording trips to Kahiki, and the Hawaiian Islands evolved in isolation from the rest of Polynesia (Kirch 2010a: 87–8, see below).

Figure 3 View of the Waipiʻo Valley, a classic amphitheatre-headed windward Polynesian valley which would have had high agricultural potential but is also prone to flooding, as noted in the Moʻikeha saga.

The arrival of human beings into new island environments left indelible marks both in the form of evidence for settlement and transformed ecologies. Common patterns associated with human settlement in Polynesia include large-scale deforestation and extinction or extirpation (local elimination) of bird and mammal species. These processes occurred both because of direct human interventions (hunting, clearing land for gardening), but also competition from commensal species, above all the Pacific rat (*Rattus exulans*). Humans also brought a 'transported landscape' of domesticated plants and animals. The main crop species in ancestral Polynesia included bananas (*Musa* sp.), taro (*Colocasia esculenta*), yams (*Dioscorea* sp.), sugarcane (*Saccharum* sp.), and breadfruit (*Artocarpus altilis*), along with the ritually important intoxicant kava (*Piper methysticum*; Figure 4). Animals included pigs, dogs, and chickens, though there is also some argument that rats were 'semi-intentional' and were eaten both at sea and once people were well-established on islands (Kirch and Green 2001: 120–62; Kirch and O'Day 2003; Swift et al. 2018).

The islands of Mangareva, located about 1,500 km southeast of Tahiti, currently have a depauperate landscape that reflects a history of seabird population collapse and anthropogenic vegetation change over the last 1,000 years

Figure 4 A typical Oceanic irrigated garden plot featuring taro, vegetables, sugarcane, and kava. While still functioning, the stone terrace walls are estimated to be at least 300 years old. Futuna Island, Vanuatu.

(Kirch et al. 2015). Kirch (1997b) contrasts the complex 'arboriculture' of the Polynesian Outlier of Tikopia against the intensive monocropping, erosion, and deforestation of Mangaia in the Cook Islands. These environmental histories relate to the different historical trajectories on the two islands; one saw the emergence of a sustainable human-created ecosystem that functioned within the geographically limited and remote Tikopia; the other saw spiralling warfare and social terror under extreme resource stress in Mangaia.

Pacific Islands and their inhabitants have long been used as metaphors or microcosms for human histories, especially environmental histories (Kirch 2007). Perhaps the most striking example is Rapa Nui, famous for the *moai*, massive carved-stone images scattered among the island's barren grasslands. Diamond (2005) used Rapa Nui in his popular work on 'collapse', arguing that the Rapanui (indigenous people of Rapa Nui) 'chose' to deforest their island while focusing instead on their monumental constructions. More recent arch-aeological work fundamentally undermines the premise of Diamond's argu-ment. Far from a metaphor for reckless human stupidity and destructiveness, Rapa Nui represents processes of environmental learning and adaptation to one of the world's most challenging continuously occupied human environments.

Hunt and Lipo (2009) specifically take Diamond to task on three main fronts. First, the primary culprits for the deforestation of Rapa Nui were not people, but rats, and they point to direct evidence of palm nuts showing the distinctive markings left by rat teeth. Second, Diamond's assumptions about the history of population on the island is out of step with current archaeological evidence. Put simply, Diamond places the initial settlement of the islands too early, as well as the apparent demographic decline, which is now understood to date to after European contact and thus results from introduced diseases rather than some kind of internal societal breakdown. Likewise, while predation of seabirds by humans and rats would have impacted soil chemistry, the erosion and mass wasting seen at present on the island is a result of Spanish ranching and the introduction of sheep and cattle, which cause major damage to Rapa Nui's soil profile.

Subsequent research has found even more compelling evidence that, rather than passively watching their environment decline, Rapanui continued to actively manage and invest in their environment even as it became increasingly deforested. New evidence has revealed extensive 'rock gardens', intentional scatters of basaltic stone that simultaneously acted as windbreaks for the staple starchy crops (primarily the sweet potato) and returned nutrients to the soil as the rocks decayed (Ladefoged et al. 2013; Stevenson et al. 2002; Wozniak 1999). Newly recovered evidence shows that Rano Raraku, the main quarry for the famed *moai*, was also located in Rapa Nui's agricultural 'sweet spot', suggesting some of the statues were at least at some point tied to a cult of crop fertility (Sherwood et al. 2019). Clearly the 'collapse' narrative can be substantially revised based on this evidence if we imagine Rapa Nui's pre-European history as a garden island, rather than a human-made wasteland.

The Hawaiian Islands are the world's most geographically isolated archipelago. One result of this isolation was the development of a high degree of biodiversity, emblematic of which are the flightless *Nēnē* (*Branta sandwicensis*), descendants of Canada geese blown off course in a storm who found a tolerable climate with no predators. Unfortunately, biodiverse ecosystems that develop in isolation are also extremely vulnerable to species extirpation and extinction resulting from human activities (Vitousek 2018). As elsewhere in the Pacific, humans and rats in Hawai'i caused extinction or extirpation of numerous plant and bird species within the first century or so of human colonisation (Athens 2009).

At the same time, Hawaiians began extensively clearing land for agriculture. As the population grew, Hawai'i developed a distinctively intensive form of agriculture involving both rain-fed and irrigated systems (Ladefoged et al. 2009, 2011; McCoy and Graves 2010). Over time agricultural practices had impacts on soil fertility (Vitousek et al. 2004). People reacted to stresses on the system by dividing and subdividing field systems over time, as is evident in the massive Leeward Kohala Field System of Hawai'i Island (Kirch 2011).

Perhaps the most dramatic case of human-induced extinction in Oceania comes from Aotearoa (New Zealand), home to the enormous, flightless *moa*, the largest of which (*Dinornis giganteus*) stood at up to 4 m in height. The discovery of stone tools with the massive bird bones in 1872 led the geologist Julian Van Haast (1872) to posit a '*moa* hunter' culture that pre-dated the extant Māori. Van Haast was mistaken in the sense that the prehistoric *moa* hunters were in fact the ancestors of Māori people, but the discovery of human-induced extinctions of native animals was nonetheless a momentous one in the history of Pacific archaeology. More recent research by Holdaway et al. (2014) has added a remarkable facet to this story, showing that the human population that caused the *moa* extinction was extremely small and dispersed, at less than 0.01 people per square kilometre, and this event happened very quickly, over a span of about fifty years, or roughly two human generations.

As elsewhere in Oceania, Aotearoa emphasises the fragility of island ecosystems during initial human settlement. Many more vertebrate species went extinct during the early period of Māori habitation of Aotearoa, and the islands also saw widespread deforestation (Anderson 2002). Human incursion drove the extirpation of New Zealand fur seals from the North Island in the early years of Māori occupation, and the species nearly went extinct because of European sealing activities. The subsequent 'rebound' of fur seal populations is an example of species resilience once human predation for meat, fat, or furs had finally ceased (Smith 2005).

Aotearoa likewise pushed the limits of the Polynesian suite of crop domesticates, basically all of which were adapted to tropical environments. The lone exception was *kumara* (sweet potato), a frost-adapted crop which the Polynesians had received from contacts with South America. Staples like yam, taro, and breadfruit could only potentially be cultivated in the subtropical north of the country, and even then not reliably or at a large scale. The rest of the country focused on the sweet potato, and in the South Island on gathering marine resources and propagation of plants that grew well in forest margins and clearings, such as bracken fern (*Pteridium esculentum*) which has an edible starchy root (Anderson 2002; Anderson et al. 2014).

Even when encountering environments that pushed the limits of the traditional resource base, Polynesian navigators sailed onwards. There is evidence for Polynesian presence on subantarctic islands such as Enderby Island in the Aucklands group, about 450 km south of the southern tip of New Zealand's South Island, around 1350CE. These extreme environments, only fifteen degrees of latitude above the Antarctic Circle, were too difficult to occupy permanently. Occupation is interpreted as lasting only a few seasons or perhaps years, after which the Auckland Islands were abandoned until Europeans returned in the nineteenth century (Anderson 2009). There is even limited evidence from oral traditions hinting that Māori navigators could have pushed further south than this, possibly reaching the continent of Antarctica over 1,000 years ago (Wehi et al. 2021). Within tropical Oceania more broadly navigators colonised islands that did not sustain long-term human settlement, such as Henderson Island. These islands with evidence for past human occupation but no people living on them at the point of European 'discovery' are sometimes known as the 'mystery islands' (Weisler 1994).

4 Navigating Inhabited Lands: The Americas and the Polynesian Outliers

In their voyages, Polynesian navigators did not only discover pristine uninhabited islands. Their journeys would also bring them into contacts with inhabited lands in two directions: to the east, the vast continents of the Americas; to the west, back into Melanesia and Micronesia to islands inhabited by people with whom they shared a degree of common ancestry. Currently the evidence is that Polynesians definitely reached the Americas, but they did not linger, choosing to return to their Oceanic world, while also making some key exchanges, particularly of domesticated plants and animals (Jones et al. 2011). To the west, voyagers would settle, usually on small or marginal islands, resulting in the formation of the Polynesian Outliers: islands with a Polynesian-speaking population but lying outside of the boundaries of the Polynesian triangle (Feinberg and Scaglion 2012). The processes of cultural change in the Polynesian Outliers were more complicated and involved, but resulted from a combination of incursion of a new population to sometimes densely inhabited areas and entanglement in local networks of kinship and exchange (Carson 2012; Flexner et al. 2019; Kirch 1984; Zinger et al. 2020).

There has been scholarly discussion about Polynesian contacts with the Americas since the nineteenth century, though there continues to be intense debate about the nature of these interactions. This is especially so in North America where people remain sceptical about whether contacts with California occurred at all (Jones and Klar 2012). Infamously, Thor Heyerdahl speculated and then set out to 'prove' that Polynesians had come from South America because of apparent similarities between Andean and Rapa Nui stonework, among other lines of 'evidence'. Even in Heyerdahl's time most archaeologists believed that the broad sweep of Polynesian navigation was from west to east (Melander 2019), and this remains the consensus today. Nonetheless, the history of misguided attempts to find connections from South America to Polynesia to some degree explains some archaeologists' reluctance to engage with the limited evidence for such contacts.

There is at least one definite line of evidence that Polynesians reached South America and made exchanges with South American people. The sweet potato (*Ipomoea batatas*), originally domesticated in the Andes mountains of South America, was transported throughout Polynesia centuries before the arrival of Spanish navigators (Yen 1974). There is direct evidence for pre-European trade of this crop in the form of carbonised tubers, which have been found in Mangaia, in the southern Cook Islands, dating no later than the end of the 1300s CE (Hather and Kirch 1991). Linguistic evidence also suggests a Polynesian dispersal of sweet potatoes, as shown by a linguistic reconstruction to Proto-Eastern Polynesian of *kūmala*, closely related to the South American name *kumar* (Yen 1974). These lines of evidence are strongly supported by genetic evidence, though subsequent re-introductions of the sweet potato by the Spanish and other colonisers has made for a slightly complicated picture (Roullier et al. 2013).

In addition to the sweet potato, there is some evidence that the bottle gourd (*Lagenaria siceraria*) was brought back from South America by Polynesian navigators, though this is less definitive than the case for the sweet potato (Clarke et al. 2006). Evidence for the other side of the exchange – what the Polynesians left behind – has been even more difficult to determine definitively. It has been suggested on the basis of genetic evidence that the chicken was originally introduced to South America from Polynesia (Storey et al. 2007, 2013), though this remains a matter of discussion (Gongora et al. 2008; Storey et al. 2008). There has also been some suggestion of human genetic exchanges based on skeletal remains from Chile (Matisoo-Smith 2011; Matisoo-Smith and Ramirez 2010). However, archaeologists still need to do further research to better document the timing and nature of these interactions at the key sites such as Mocha Island and El Arénal as well as other sites doubtless waiting to be discovered.

The evidence for Polynesian contacts with North America, specifically the Channel Islands in southern California, is even more controversial. Jones and Klar (2005, 2012) have argued that the evidence for sewn-plank canoes, distinctive shell and bone fishhook forms, and linguistic borrowing make a case for at least some limited Polynesian contact with California, with Hawai'i as the most likely candidate for the source of the voyagers. Pacific specialists have taken issue with this argument on the basis of material and chronological evidence (Anderson 2006), while California archaeologists have argued that the linguistic and archaeological evidence is insufficient, preferring an autochthonous invention of the unique canoe and fishhook forms (Arnold 2007; see response in Jones and Klar 2009). In California as in South America, Polynesian contacts remain a matter of ongoing debate and it will be interesting to see what new evidence, for or against, might appear in coming decades.

Turning to the west, Polynesian voyagers were also actively seeking new territory, though in this case it was in islands that were already populated, in some cases quite densely. By 900CE, people had been settled into Island Melanesia for many millennia, in Near Oceania since the last Ice Age. Island Melanesia during this period was undergoing a continued pattern of intensive regionalisation and diversification (Bedford 2006; Spriggs 1997; Walter and Sheppard 2017). At the same time, intensive maritime exchange networks were being established and expanded upon. Indeed, Kirch (2017: 148) considers 'development of specialised trade and exchange networks' to be 'a recurring theme in the prehistory of "New" Melanesia'.

In a sense, the incursion of Polynesians was simply an addition to ongoing patterns of inter-island voyaging, trade, intermarriage, conflict, and settlement. What is distinctive in this case is the marked linguistic divergence between the newcomers and the existing population. Outlier languages remain more closely related to those in the Polynesian phylogenetic language tree than those of the neighbouring islands (Kirch and Green 2001: 53–91). In other words, the Aniwa/Futuna language of South Vanuatu is more closely related to Hawaiian or New Zealand Māori, thousands of kilometres distant, than it is to any of the languages from the intervisible islands of Erromango, Tanna, or Aneityum, reachable by a few hours in a sailing canoe and which are themselves quite linguistically distinctive from each other. At the same time there is abundant evidence for linguistic exchange and borrowing. In southern Vanuatu, language for the consumption of kava and ritual beliefs and practices relating to the main deities *Mwatiktiki* and *Tangalua* on Tanna are clear borrowings from Polynesian language and custom (Lindstrom 2004; Lynch 1996). Meanwhile, on the nearby Outlier of West Futuna, the chiefly system uses the structure and names of the two Tannese 'moieties', *Namruke* and *Kaviameta* (Flexner et al. 2018a: 252; Keller and Kuautonga 2007: 61).

The Polynesian Outliers have been a long-standing matter of interest in Pacific archaeology, linguistics, and anthropology. Early debates centred on the question of origins: were the Outliers remnant populations of ancient Polynesian speakers in areas overwritten by a subsequent 'Melanesian' migration; or were they a result of a 'backwash' migration from Polynesia some time in later prehistory? The consensus for the last thirty-five years has been that the latter case is the most parsimonious explanation: Polynesian voyagers moving west, probably from the vicinity of Western Polynesia, including Tonga and

Samoa, and most likely within the last 1,000 years (see Carson 2012; Kirch 1984). A recent analysis of imported obsidian artefacts from Tikopia in the Solomon Islands provided direct evidence of voyaging from Tonga beginning around 1200CE, indicating a sea voyage of over 1,800 km (McCoy et al. 2020). It is notable that several of the Outliers, including West Futuna in Vanuatu and 'Uvea in the Loyalty Islands, share names with islands on the other side of the Polynesia/Melanesia boundary. Wilson (2018) offers a provocative hypothesis for these islands on linguistic grounds: that the settlement of Eastern Polynesia transited through the Outliers themselves. In other words, the people who first sailed to the Society Islands and possibly beyond came not from the 'ancestral homelands' in Western Polynesia, but from Outliers such as Rennell and Bellona in the Solomon Islands. Here again future archaeological research will play a key role as Rennell and Bellona remain relative unknowns in the field (Poulsen 1972), as do several other Outliers in the region.

One of the remarkable things about the Polynesian Outliers, beyond the epic voyages they must represent, is the diversity of their histories. In some cases, Polynesians settled on uninhabited islands, as appears to have been the case for Anuta in the southeast Solomon Islands (Kirch and Rosendahl 1973). In other cases, the islands were already inhabited and oral traditions as well as archaeology attest to cultural changes as well as admixture. On Tikopia, also in the southeast Solomons, Kirch and Yen (1982: 331–4) defined a 'Tuakamali' phase beginning around 1200CE marked by the disappearance of pottery, and distinctive new stone adze and shell fishhook forms (see also Kirch and Swift 2017). In Taumako, the 'Namu' phase from 1000CE reflects a mixture of Polynesian and non-Polynesian traits based on skeletal evidence, with the most direct evidence for Polynesian contacts appearing in the form of stone adzes sourced to the Tutuila quarry in Samoa, nearly 2,500 km away (Leach and Davidson 2008: 297–9; 305). In the southern Outliers in Vanuatu and New Caledonia there is little definitive material evidence for Polynesian arrival, despite the clear linguistic distinction (Flexner et al. 2019).

Evidence for what actually happened when Polynesia re-encountered Melanesia is likewise somewhat varied. That the Outliers are generally located on smaller, often remote or marginal islands suggests that they were formed by relatively small groups of people compared with the extant local populations (e.g., Flexner et al. 2018a). Nonetheless, these relatively small populations were able to affect major linguistic and cultural changes, possibly because of the prestige of the larger exchange networks they drew upon, or the new supernatural practices and beliefs they imported to the islands. There was certainly conflict, as has been noted in Tikopia oral traditions (Firth 1961), but there is also abundant evidence for intermarriage and the integration of the newcomers into local trade and exchange networks, for example, between Taumako and Santa Cruz (Leach and Davidson 2008: 319–22).

A result of these entanglements was arguably the emergence of a 'hybrid' identity. 'The Outliers were not simply home to Polynesians who lived outside of the triangle' (Flexner et al. 2019: 420). Rather, they were a result of something new: processes of exchange and interaction among people with some marked differences in language, material culture, and belief, but also shared practices as maritime people adapted to life on islands. For example, the shared agricultural regime and similar foodways (the cultivation, harvesting, preparing, and consuming of the Pacific suite of food crops, seafood, and domesticated animals) reflect the shared ancestry that Pacific Islanders can trace back over thousands of years.

5 Political Epics in Island Societies

For New Zealand Māori, *whakapapa* (usually translated as 'genealogy' but also encompassing more-than-human relationships across space and time; see Marshall 2021) is an important way of recounting historical events, important cultural truths, as well as ongoing ties to place and kinship. Māori trace their heritage in *iwi* ('tribes') and *hapū* ('clans') that go back to named *waka* (canoes) which are now accepted as an actual fleet of canoes that carried the first Polynesians to Aotearoa (see Mead 2003; Taunui 2015; Walker 1990). Archaeological research on the earliest dates for settlement in New Zealand, now narrowed to a span of a few decades ca. 1250CE (see Dye 2015; Horsburgh and McCoy 2017: 7; Wilmshurst et al. 2011) accords remarkably well with estimates based on the *whakapapa* genealogies that trace back to the original *waka*. This is not to say that archaeology's main job is to prove or disprove what is recorded in oral traditions, but that these different lines of evidence provide complementary information to each other (see Flexner 2014b; Kirch 2018). For example, Walter et al. (2017) propose that the evidence for settlement impacts in the fourteenth century CE reflects a period of mass migration and systematic colonisation resulting from a concerted movement of people from tropical Polynesia to Aotearoa that accords with traditional accounts.

Beyond initial settlement in New Zealand, Māori oral traditions relate to cycles of settlement, conflict, and the movement of people and resources around the landscape. As populations expanded people settled into the landscape, particularly on the North Island (Figure 5). Access to sources of stone for tools, particularly volcanic glass, led to more restricted exchange networks as particular groups limited access to certain sources to themselves and their allies (McCoy and Carpenter 2014; McCoy et al. 2014). As conflict over resources

Figure 5 Example of a terraced landscape typical of the areas of New Zealand's
North Island where Pā are located, Bay of Plenty region.

and territory intensified, warfare between rival groups occasionally broke out.
Māori constructed monumental hillforts, known as Pā, which served as places
of agricultural storage, habitation, ancestral ritual, and, when needed, defence.
However, the emergence of these sites was not simply a question of geography
or environment. Rather, oral traditions speak to specific events that structure the
way that conflict shaped the landscape across time and space (Bedford 2013;
Campbell 2008; Philips 2000). Māori concepts like *mana* (power or prestige)
and *utu* (revenge) are equally important when understanding the patterns of
historical territoriality, chiefly politics, and warfare in Aotearoa.

A landmark study in Oceania that combined archaeology and oral traditions
was the French archaeologist Jose Garanger's (1972, 1996) research in central
Vanuatu (then called the New Hebrides/Nouvelles Hébrides). Garanger became
fascinated with stories about the great chief Roi Mata, as well as a major
eruption that destroyed a no-longer-extant island called Kuwae. Working with
local informants and knowledge-keepers, Garanger was able to excavate Roi
Mata's main home village at Mangaas, as well as his burial place at Retoka
Island. He discovered that the archaeological evidence from over 500 years ago
matched specific details from the oral traditions, especially concerning the
nature of Roi Mata's death and burial. Garanger also found evidence for

a massive volcanic eruption based on tephra deposits that could be directly dated using radioactive isotopes. The Kuwae eruption is now known to be one of the three largest volcanic events in the last 1,000 years, and has been securely dated to 1452CE (Robin et al. 1994).

Stories about Roi Mata and Kuwae are present across the north of Efate Island and the neighbouring Shepherds group. While there are general commonalities, Ballard (2016) has also noted that stories can vary from community to community, particularly where there are ongoing political motivations to accept one version as the 'true' story of Roi Mata. What is known is that Roi Mata was a very powerful paramount chief, who was particularly renowned for his diplomatic skills, negotiating a major peace agreement between the warring chiefdoms of Efate and neighbouring islands. Yet Roi Mata was also aware of the danger of concentrating power too much, and on his death, rather than establishing a hereditary dynasty, he allowed his influence to die with him. His burial is marked by massive upright coral slabs, and Garanger's excavations revealed that Roi Mata was indeed buried with his most powerful warriors, wives, and retainers (see Garanger 1972; Spriggs 1997: 207–12). What remained was a stable heterarchy of chiefly cooperation that lasted for several centuries, arguably until the present day.

Decades or possibly centuries after Roi Mata's death, there was the major Kuwae eruption. According to Spriggs (1997: 212–17), the eruption is remembered as being caused by a man called Tombuk or Toboka, a powerful sorcerer who was tricked by the people of Kuwae into committing incest with his mother. In revenge, he caused a devastating cataclysm on the island (see Ballard 2020 for another version of the story). The only survivors were some chiefs who escaped by canoe to Efate, and a boy and a girl: Asingmet and Tarifeget. Asingmet would go on to become a powerful chief in his own right, achieving the title of Ti Tongoa Liseiriki. Like Roi Mata, Ti Tongoa Liseiriki's burial place is known, and he was also buried with wives and retainers. Ti Tongoa Liseiriki had four pig-tusk bracelets, but was only buried with three, having passed on the fourth along with the title of Roi Mata to a chief named Mwasoe Nua whose monumental group burial was also excavated by Garanger. Many scholars have speculated about the 'Polynesian' influences of some of these chiefly histories, which have structural similarities to those of Polynesian chiefdoms and coincide with the time of the formation of Polynesian Outliers in Vanuatu (Ballard 2016; Guiart 1982, 2013).

In the south of Vanuatu, there are likewise chiefly epics including titles that are passed on today. On the island of Aneityum, early clearing of the uplands led to mass erosion, resulting in the formation of alluvial sediment fans in the stream valleys. Aneityumese people took advantage of this geological accident by constructing massive systems of canals and pondfields for growing taro. Because of the greater need to control resources and manage labour in these systems, the people who were able to exert their authority to create the new chiefly order created a new form of paramount title, *Natimarid* (Spriggs 1981). Aneityum can be contrasted with the more fractious and heterarchical neighbouring island of Tanna, along with the neighbouring Polynesian Outliers of Futuna and Aniwa (Spriggs 1986; Flexner 2021). Another oral tradition from the south of Vanuatu relates to the founding of the Xetriwaan Dynasty, an important chiefly lineage in the Loyalty Islands of New Caledonia, from Aneityum representing a journey of roughly 300 km (Spriggs 1997: 219–20).

On Tanna, chiefly titles involve what Lindstrom (2011) calls the 'Heroic I'. Holding a title not only reflects an individual's accomplishments, but also the accomplishments of all previous holders of that title. One such chiefly name from the south of Tanna Island is Iarisi, who was responsible for the relationship between the *neteta* (land division) around his home village of Kwaraka and the neighbouring island of Aneityum. His title was *yani en dete*, a 'guardian of social well-being and local values and practices' (Douglas 1996: 243). Excavations at Iarisi's village (Figure 6) recovered some evidence of the historically recorded encounter with Presbyterian missionaries, which was facilitated by Iarisi in the 1850s, but also longer-term evidence for feasting going back at least into the 1600s (Flexner et al. 2016). The name of Iarisi is still passed on among South Tanna chiefs, an ongoing tradition of leadership stretching back over 400 years.

To the west of Vanuatu lies the New Caledonia archipelago, consisting of the large continental island of La Grande Terre and surrounding smaller islands including the Loyalty Islands to the east and Île des Pins to the south. New Caledonia's traditional Kanak societies were classified by Europeans as typical of the 'big men' type, with a relatively egalitarian structure in which status was achieved rather than inherited. Archaeological research has shown that the apparent small-scale and horizontal organisation of Kanak societies as recorded by European ethnographers results from societal upheaval and reorganisation due to demographic decline and displacement from traditional lands during the time of European colonialism. Archaeological surveys have uncovered extensive evidence for monumental earthworks, including large aggregated villages consisting of hundreds of house mounds, platforms, and terraces. Material culture including pottery and stone tools also indicates complex material exchange networks dating to the last 1,000 years or more (Sand 1996, 2002; Sand et al. 2003).

North of Vanuatu in the Solomon Islands lies the large, high island of New Georgia. Roviana lagoon, situated along the southern coast of this island,

Figure 6 Excavating a 350-year-old mound containing the remains of a communal feast from Iarisi's traditional village, Anuikaraka, Tanna, Vanuatu.

features a dense concentration of resources including rich garden soils, marine resources, and fossil tridacna shells in raised extinct coral reefs, which was key to the manufacture of shell valuables (Walter et al. 2004). A chiefdom focused on the construction of stone monuments, the exchange of shell valuables, and headhunting emerged in Roviana around the 1600s CE. Oral traditions recount the story of Ididubanara, an inland chief from Bao who invaded Roviana lagoon with his people and established a dynastic chiefdom in the area. Roviana's chiefs would go on to dominate the Western Solomons for several centuries (Sheppard 2019).

By the nineteenth century, Roviana chiefs were able to monopolise the incoming trade opportunities with Europeans, particularly of iron hatchets, which only intensified headhunting practice (Thomas 2019). This colonial-era dominance has shaped perceptions of relationships between coastal 'saltwater' and inland 'bush' people in the larger islands of the Solomons. The bush here, as elsewhere in Island Melanesia, was largely uninhabited by the twentieth century. However, research by Bayliss-Smith et al. (2019) has revealed evidence for intensive taro cultivation in irrigated field systems since at least the 1600s CE, if not earlier. They suggest the origins of headhunting and shrine construction in the Roviana chiefdoms might have in fact been a response to the large quantities of taro the inland field systems were producing for politically significant competitive feasts. As with so much of Island Melanesia, while there has been great progress in recent decades, this is an area where more research is needed to better understand the timing and nature of the evolution of these systems, and the relationships with the other neighbouring islands.

Moving east into Polynesia, the islands of Tonga were home to the region's most expansive 'maritime empire'. Beginning around the mid-1400s CE, Tongan chiefs from the island of Tongatapu increasingly centralised and solidified their authority and control. Commoners were alienated from control over land rights, becoming tributary serfs. The chiefly class was split, with the creation of a class of 'small chiefs' (*hou'eiki*) charged with collecting tribute to serve the paramount Tuʻi Tonga, a semi-divine ruler, and his immediate family. These social transformations were matched with the development of new forms of monumental architecture, including a massive complex of stone tombs called *langi*, and associated altars and mounds. The royal burial complex at Lapaha is constructed in an area of reclaimed land, including a massive ditch and drainage system adjacent to a purpose-built harbour for large sailing canoes (Clark et al. 2008).

The expansion of the Tongan maritime empire is reflected in the archaeology of neighbouring islands. In the north of the modern Kingdom of Tonga is the island of Niuatoputapu, which Kirch (1988) suggests was relatively independent but by the sixteenth century CE was increasingly dominated by the expansive dominion of the Tuʻi Tonga. Similar arguments have been made for ʻUvea Island (Sand 1998). Recent analyses of stone artefacts from archaeological sites in Tongatapu revealed a significant increase in stone imports after the emergence of the Tongan state, a proxy for inter-island exchange. Samoa, including the islands of Savaiʻi, ʻUpolu, and Tutuila, was a particularly prominent source of adzes and other stone imports (Clark et al. 2014).

Kirch and Yen (1982: 331–4, 341–3) identified clear material transformation during the Polynesian Outlier Tikopia's Tuakamali phase which correlates with Polynesian settlement of the island. Evidence from oral traditions (Firth 1961) indicates multiple Tikopian lineages originating in Polynesia.

The highest-ranking chiefly lineages are traced to Tonga. Analysis of volcanic glass sources reinforces the perspective of Tikopia as an Outlier entangled in the Tongan Empire. Early artefacts from roughly 2,850 years ago are sourced to the south and west in Vanuatu and the Admiralty Islands, with imports declining through time. Around 1250CE, while there was continued import of volcanic glass from Vanuatu, a small amount of imported material can be sourced to Tonga. Direct voyages between Tonga and Tikopia are interpreted as uncommon as the amount of Tongan volcanic glass is small. This is nonetheless seen as evidence of a strategy of Tongan expansion by settling chiefly families and establishing lineages on islands that would be drawn into the sphere of influence of the Tu'i Tonga (McCoy et al. 2020).

Samoa was part of the Tongan maritime exchange network, while maintaining its own system of complex chiefly life and lineages. A common feature in the Samoan landscape are mounds of earth and stone, including the 'star mounds' identified in the earliest archaeological surveys of the archipelago. There is also a variety of house mounds as well as mounds for the chiefly sport of pigeon snaring, which were called *tia seu lupe* (see Green and Davidson 1974). Spatial analysis of the locations of mounds in the islands of Savai'i and 'Upolu based on current survey data has revealed a strong association between the density of these features and agricultural potential, particularly for growing rain-fed taro (Glover et al. 2020). As on Rapa Nui and other parts of Polynesia, monumental construction correlates with the best agricultural land in the islands.

Among the largest mound sites in Samoa are Pulemelei and Laupele. Pulemelei on the island of Savai'i is believed to be the largest freestanding stone structure in Western Polynesia. The mound, made of local volcanic stone, is over 60 m across at the base and 40 m across at the top, rising up to 12 m above the ground surface. It was built in three phases, beginning roughly 1100–1300CE, with the final level of the mound coinciding with a pinnacle in chiefly rituals around 1400–1600CE (Martinsson-Wallin et al. 2007). Laupele, located on the island of 'Upolu, measures over 100 m across at its base, and rises to a height of 12 m. People would have had to move over 45,000 m^3 of earth and stone by hand to build the mound. Archaeological excavations at Laupele did not find suitable material for radiocarbon dating, but the presence of a distinctive type of stone adze and associated evidence suggest the period when the largest mounds were built dates to 700–900 years ago. Laupele is associated with the *Tafa'ifa* chiefly title in oral traditions. Both Pulemelei and Laupele are argued to represent activities associated with chiefly ritual, prestige, and power during a time when Samoan society was more hierarchical than it is at present (Martinsson-Wallin 2014).

Western Pacific interactions led to a process of 'polygenesis' in Fiji, which features a few Polynesian Outliers but evolved along its own trajectory (Burley 2013). The emergence of fortifications and endemic warfare has been explained in terms of variable local resources and chiefly competition (Field 1998), which intensified in the nineteenth century with the introduction of firearms (Burley et al. 2016). However, oral traditions from Fiji also point to Tongan lineages and competition with Tonga for power and influence (Parke 2014).

In the southern Vanuatu Polynesian Outlier of Futuna, stories of connection to Tonga are mythical rather than referring to specific lineages, with the culture hero *Majihjihki* (the Polynesian demi-god Maui) making multiple voyages in pursuit of his Tongan wives (Keller and Kuautonga 2007: 146–65). This leaves open the possibility that rather than a situation of political dominance by Tongan interlopers, the southern Vanuatu Polynesian Outliers resulted from processes of cultural hybridisation (Flexner et al. 2019). It is even possible there is a history of resistance to centralised authority in these islands, particularly as the chiefly systems of Futuna and Aniwa followed the more horizontally organised heterarchies of neighbouring Tanna (Flexner 2021: 209–10; Flexner et al. 2018a: 249–53). Like all empires, Tonga had its competitors and enclaves of 'non-state space' at the limits of its geopolitical influence (see Scott 2009).

The other 'archaic states' in Polynesia emerged in the Hawaiian kingdoms (Kirch 2010a). As noted above, Hawai'i is the most geographically isolated archipelago in the Pacific. There was an early period of inter-island voyaging between Hawai'i and Central Polynesia, known from oral traditions (e.g., Kamakau 1991: 3–5; Malo 1951: 7–10) as well as archaeological evidence (Collerson and Weisler 2007). However, beginning around 1400CE voyaging ceased and the Hawaiian chiefdoms were essentially isolated from the rest of the world until contact with the British in 1778. Hawai'i's 'Late Expansion' and 'Proto-Historic' periods (see Kirch and McCoy 2007) included a remarkable expansion and intensification of agricultural and aquacultural systems, emergence of new forms of political organisation, and construction of a monumental temple system to provide ideological justification for divine kingship.

As with other Oceanic chiefdoms, the agricultural base for Hawaiian society lay in the cultivation of taro (*kalo*), primarily in irrigated pondfields, and rainfed gardens focused primarily on the introduced American cultigen the sweet potato (*'uala*). These crops were supplemented with bananas, breadfruit, sugarcane, and the elite intoxicant kava (*'awa*). Soils and rainfall circumscribed the areas where different kinds of agriculture were possible (Ladefoged et al. 2009). Over time, increasingly marginal areas saw intensification of agricultural use, resulting in smaller and more elaborate walled field systems through time. Rainfed examples include the North Kohala field system on Hawai'i Island (e.g.,

Ladefoged et al. 2003; Kirch 2011) and the Kalaupapa field system of Molokai (McCoy 2005). Irrigated systems included those of Halelea, Kaua'i (Earle 1978), Hālawa, Molokai (Kirch and Kelly 1975), and Anahulu, O'ahu, a system that was redeveloped when the Hawaiian Kingdoms transformed yet again following European contact (Spriggs 1992). New forms of agricultural terracing and water distribution systems were also created as commoners (*maka 'āinana*) came under increasing pressure to provide tribute to chiefs and royals (McCoy and Graves 2010). To better harvest the seas, Hawaiians created monumental fish traps along coastal margins, some covering areas of over a square kilometre, as is the case for several examples from Molokai (Summers 1971).

Scaling up from the field systems, the need to organise agricultural production also shaped the territorial organisation of the Hawaiian Islands (Ladefoged and Graves 2006). The basic unit of land was the *ahupua'a*, a wedge-shaped division meant to provide an extended kin group with a variety of resources from mountain to sea. As with the garden plots, these divisions became smaller and smaller through time. Several *ahupua'a* would be organised into a *moku* (district), and the district chief was referred to as the *ali'i 'ai moku* (literally 'the chief who eats the district'). Eventually a new chiefly title, *mō'i* (king), would be created for the *ali'i nui* (big chief) of the *mokupuni*, which Kirch (2010a: 46–8) argues was a form of archaic state. Accompanying this shift was a proliferation of lesser titles for lower-ranking chiefs (*ali'i*), managers (*konohiki*), and ritual specialists (*kahuna*). The names and deeds of several *ali'i nui*, such as Mā'ilikūkahi of O'ahu Island, 'Umi-a-Līloa of Hawai'i Island, and Pi'ikea of Maui, are passed down through the Hawaiian oral traditions. As with the motivations for voyaging, a common factor in the establishment of royal lineages was a junior sibling who controlled the war god Kū (see Kirch 2010a: 88–121 for a summary). Kamehameha, one such junior sibling and eventually the *mō'i* or king who unified the islands under a single hereditary dynasty, is known both from oral traditions and the documentary record since his conquests occurred during the period of early European contacts in the Hawaiian Islands (see Kamakau 1991: 89–122; Kuykendall 1965: 29–60; Sahlins 1992: 38–45).

As in Tonga, the rise of the *mō'i* was accompanied with an increase in construction of monumental stone structures, which in Hawai'i were primarily the *heiau*, stone temples constructed for the worship of gods, most prominently Lono, the god of fertility, and Kū, the god of war (Figure 7). The construction of *heiau* of particular forms is associated with the emergence of more elaborate chiefly hierarchy and a supporting priestly class (Kirch 2010a: 156–76; Kolb 2006). *Heiau* were oriented to particular directions, including in relation to the rising and setting of the constellation Pleiades (*Makali'i*) which marked the

Figure 7 Puʻukoholā, the *luakini heiau* (war temple) where the *aliʻi nui*
Kamehameha sacrificed his cousin in 1791CE, beginning his conquest of
unification of the Hawaiian Islands.

important *Makahiki* ritual cycle (Kirch 2004; McCoy 2014). The expansionistic
Maui Island Kingdom featured a variety of *heiau* forms, including a distinctive
'notched' feature found in neighbouring islands where the Maui kings held
sway (Kirch and Ruggles 2019).

As Dye (2010) has argued, the alienation of *makaʻāinana* (commoners) and
increasing centralisation of power and wealth in a chiefly class is reflected in
archaeological evidence for reduction in quality of oven stones and timber for
cooking fires through time among commoner households. The *kapu* system
determined relationships between genders, classes of people, and arrangement
of domestic and ritual spaces. While in theory *kapu* was hegemonic for
Hawaiian people, evidence from *makaʻāinana* households suggests it was
more flexibly interpreted in some families (McCoy and Codlin 2017). *Aliʻi*,
who lived in more elaborate houses, were able to differentiate gendered and
sacred spaces more rigidly (Field et al. 2010; Weisler and Kirch 1985).
Members of the priestly class (*kahuna*) also had domestic spaces that materially
reflected their special status in Hawaiian society (Kirch et al. 2010).

Returning west, and into Micronesia, the island of Pohnpei features one of the
most elaborate and remarkable stone constructions in Oceania (to view a 3D

model of one of the burial features, visit https://sketchfab.com/3d-models/bur ial-monument-nan-madol-pohnpei-micronesia-3843a0781c1e41ccbf95 f784a7b71f92). The site of Nan Madol was the centre of chiefly power and mausoleum of the Saudeleur Dynasty, which ruled from approximately 1200 to 1600CE. It consists of a series of 130 structures built on 98 artificial islands (McCoy et al. 2015). The monumental structures feature a distinctive construction technique using prismatic basalt columns connected by a system of interlocking canals and sea walls. Analysis of the massive stones, many of which are 2–3 m in length and weigh thousands of kilograms, shows they were transported from a quarry on the opposite side of the island, a distance of roughly 12 km (McCoy et al. 2016).

Recent survey of the areas adjacent to Nan Madol using a technique called light detection and ranging (LiDAR) revealed an extensive terraced cultivation system (Comer et al. 2019) that likely provided the agrarian background for the rise of the Saudeleur. The end of the Saudeleur Dynasty is recorded in detailed oral traditions. The last of the Saudeleur attempted to capture one of the gods, Nan Sapwe, who escaped. Nan Sapwe had a son called Isokelekel, who returned to earth with 333 warriors. Flying in from the east, Isokelekel and his warriors overthrew the ruler and introduced the current chiefly system of Nahmwarki and Nahnken (see Kirch 2017: 177–8).

Other examples of monumental construction associated with political competition abound in Micronesia. On the island of Guam in the Marianas group, Chamorro people built their houses on top of paired rows of massive stone pillars known as *latte*. *Latte* stones can reach up to 5 m in height. The largest arrangements have up to fourteen pairs of *latte*. *Latte* sites consist of aggregations of these structures, with the largest houses taking up a central location. The earliest periods of *latte* construction date to between 1000 and 1300CE, though they continued to be built up to the period of Spanish colonisation in the 1600s CE (Athens 2011). There remains some debate about the amount of hierarchy in Chamorro society in the past, with some scholars arguing that the higher and larger houses belonged to higher-ranked individuals (Graves 1986), while others suggest a more horizontal distribution of wealth and power (Craib 1986; see also Kirch 2017: 165–7).

The tiny island group of Yap, with a total landmass of less than 100 km^2, consists of four islands separated by narrow water passages with a shared reef. Beginning around 1400CE, sailors from Yap began travelling to the Palau archipelago, 450 km to the southwest, to quarry limestone to make massive discs called *rai* (stone money). *Rai* stones can be over 4.5 m in diameter, and the heaviest weigh over eight metric tons. The transport of thousands of *rai* from Palau to Yap, which continued through the period of Japanese occupation in the

1940s, represents long-distance transport of the largest and heaviest objects ever carried on traditional Oceanic sailing canoes. However, the value of *rai* lay not exclusively in their size or appearance, but rather in the social relationships and lineages they represented through oral traditions recounting previous owners and exchanges (Fitzpatrick 2003; Fitzpatrick and McKeon 2019). This kind of relational approach to exchange is a hallmark of many Oceanic societies (see Strathern 1990).

6 Oceania Encounters Europe

The period between roughly 1000 and 1800CE saw a great proliferation of new forms of political organisation, religious belief, and architectural innovation throughout the Oceanic region. As Europeans began entering the scene in the 1500s, these forms would further evolve both as a result of new introductions, and indigenous adaptability, resilience, and creativity. Between 1513 and 1779, the Pacific Ocean went from a blank or largely imagined space on European maps, to one where most of the islands had been accurately charted and visited. For the most part, contacts between European navigators and Islanders were brief or fleeting, though these encounters with strangers from across the horizon did in many cases have lasting effects. Some islands saw regular encounters with Europeans from the sixteenth century onwards, such as in the Solomon Islands. Other groups, such as the Hawaiian Islands, remained completely isolated from European encounter until towards the end of the eighteenth century, complicating the notion of a 'contact period' for Oceania (Flexner 2014a: 48–53).

The ability to access written records, charts, and illustrations offers greater opportunity to follow specific historical events and individuals. However, one of the main benefits of a critical reading of these sources for Pacific historical anthropology is the opportunity to gain insights into the nature of Islander societies, and what early moments of contact threw into relief, shaping subsequent perceptions on both sides of the beaches where these events took place (see Dening 1980, 2004). As Spriggs (1997: 223) points out, rather than representing a 'break' with a pre-European era, early contacts in Melanesian Islands as well as other parts of Oceania were likely perceived as a continuation of the Polynesian incursions of the previous five centuries.

By 1500CE, Spain was in the process of transitioning out of its own 'Middle Ages', from a peripheral, politically fractious frontier to an expansive empire in its own right (MacKay 1977). The first European to sight the Pacific was the Spanish explorer Vasco Nuñez de Balboa in 1513. In the preceding decades the Spanish had both established an imperial foothold in the Americas and established dominions in Maluku and the Spice Islands, which offered a lucrative trade. At the time Portugal and Spain were in the midst of a territorial dispute concerning which half of the world these islands occupied, and thus who had the right to colonise them following the division of the world under the Treaty of Tordesillas (Spate 2004 [1979]: 27–9). In an atmosphere of high courtly intrigue and international rivalry, a Portuguese-born navigator named Fernão de Magalhães (Ferdinand Magellan) was given the Spanish royal standard and blessing to set sail for the Spice Islands, voyaging from east to west (Beaglehole 1966: 15–22).

Magellan set sail in 1519 with a fleet of five ships, finally arriving in the Pacific via the straits at the southern tip of South America that bear his name in November 1520. The voyage included an attempted mutiny that was put down, and a successful mutiny that resulted in one of the ships, the *San Antonio*, defecting and returning to Spain during the crossing from Atlantic to Pacific. The journey Magellan led across the Pacific saw extreme hardship, with the crew suffering from scurvy and starvation. Setting a bee-line for the Spice Islands from the west coast of South America, Magellan's fleet passed surprisingly few islands, and the ones it did pass were not deemed promising sources for produce or fresh water. The fleet only stopped on 6 March 1521 in islands Magellan dubbed the *Ladrones* ('thieves') after the inhabitants stole the skiff of the *Trinidad* (the islands are Guam and Rota in the southern Marianas; Beaglehole 1966: 23–32). In retaliation, Magellan burned a village and killed several islanders before sailing onwards, establishing a pattern that would, tragically, repeat itself over the history of European voyaging in the Pacific.

Magellan sailed onwards, eventually arriving with his ailing crew in the Philippines. At the island of Cebu, he became entangled in a local dispute. On 26 April, Magellan was killed during a skirmish while a native village burned. The remaining crew sailed onwards with much diminished numbers, with only two of the ships, *Trinidad* and *Victoria*, eventually arriving back in Europe to Portugal and Spain, respectively. The first global circumnavigation claimed the lives of over 170 people, including Magellan's (Beaglehole 1966: 33–6).

While the political and economic benefits of Magellan's voyage may have been questionable, it did provide Spain with evidence that cross-Pacific voyages were possible, and that there were in fact lands and people in the great ocean, albeit widely scattered. Additional ships were dispatched to the region, with some of the earliest contacts resulting from unsuccessful attempts to voyage from the Spice Islands to the Americas by Álvaro de Saavedra Cerón in 1528 and 1529. These resulted in interactions with Islanders from Murai, part of the Manus group in northern New Guinea, including three men who were kidnapped and taken back to Maluku then returned to their island (Spriggs 1997: 223–6).

It has been argued that for the next century, the Pacific was a 'Spanish Lake', seen primarily as an obstacle to be crossed between the sources of wealth in South America and the Spice Islands (Spate 2004 [1979]). From an Oceanic perspective, however, there were several notable encounters with Spanish navigators, particularly in what are now the Solomon Islands and Vanuatu. During voyages from 1567 to 1568, Alvaro de Mendaña y Neyra charted several of the main islands in the Solomons group. In 1595, Mendaña made a return voyage with a fleet of four ships. During the night of 7–8 September 1595, the *almiranta Santa Isabel* became separated from the other ships (Beaglehole 1966: 63–80). Mendaña would go on to set up a campsite at Graciosa Bay in Nendö (Santa Cruz), though the intention to establish a settlement was not successful. Ultimately the camp was abandoned after Mendaña's death and the fleet returned to Mexico (Beaglehole 1966: 70–80; Gibbs 2011: 156–7).

Archaeological investigations at Pamua, Makira Island (San Cristoval) eventually revealed the fate of the lost *almiranta* (Allen and Green 1972; Green 1973). The crew of the *Santa Isabel* maintained course, eventually landing at Makira. There the sailors set up a defensible camp on top of a ridge where they presumably intended to wait for rescue from the rest of the fleet. There is limited evidence that they established trading relationships with the local people, including the presence of Spanish pottery and a native burial with a metal aiglet in the highest mound of the neighbouring village of Mwanihuki (Gibbs 2011: 157–60). Ultimately it is not known whether the marooned crew of the *Santa Isabel*, consisting of 180 men, women, and children from throughout the Spanish Empire, were killed, starved, or incorporated into the local community.

One of the sailors in Mendaña's 1567 and 1595 voyages was Don Pedro Ferdinand de Quirós, who led the return voyage from the ill-fated settlement at Graciosa Bay. In 1600, Quirós went to Spain, where he spent several years pleading his case for another voyage to the Pacific. Quirós was convinced he would finally discover lands of infinite wealth and resources that would enrich himself and the Crown. After some misadventure on his way back to Peru, Quirós eventually departed Callao in December 1605 with a fleet of three ships provisioned by the Viceroy (Beaglehole 1966: 81–4). Again the voyage across the Pacific was marked by hardship, tensions between captain and crew, and continuous lack of fresh food and water. Eventually Quirós and crew landed at Taumako in the Solomon Islands, about 150 km northeast of Santa Cruz (Beaglehole 1966: 84–7; Spate 2004 [1979]: 134–5).

After about two weeks, during which time the expedition enjoyed friendly relationships with the local people, including a chief named Tupai, Quirós turned south in search of *Terra Australis Incognita*, the imagined great southern land of infinite riches. The expedition passed through what are now called the Banks Islands in northern Vanuatu, sighting Mere Lava and landing briefly at Gaua for fresh water (Markham 1904: 232–40). Eventually Quirós chose to settle in a large, sandy bay of an island he called *Terra Austrialia de Espritu Santo* (now simply called Espiritu Santo).

The settlement at the bay, dubbed by Quirós *Bahia de San Felipe y Santiago*, has been called a 'phantasmagoria' by historians, focusing on the religious fanaticism with which Quirós approached the fledgling settlement (Spate 2004 [1979]: 136). This should be contextualised by the ambiguities and contradictions of imperial Spain during the time (Luque and Mondragón 2005). Quirós came from a wealthy but not noble family in a religiously fervent frontier in Portugal. He was reliant on Spanish support but aligned with proto-nationalist Franciscans who believed it was a free Portugal's destiny to create a Catholic paradise on earth (Jolly 2009: 61–2).

From the Islander perspective, the would-be Spanish colonisers must have appeared as a bizarre spectacle. Quirós established a Ministry of War, and an Order of the Knights of the Holy Spirit. Much of the crew was quite ill for the duration of the 'city' of *La Nueva Jerusalem*, as Quirós called the settlement. A church was constructed of local materials, and religious festivals were the main activity in the settlement. Relationships with the local people turned sour. Attempts at interaction were met with ambush or people fleeing into the forest. After about a month, Quirós made the decision to abandon the settlement, again hoping to find grander lands to the south. The fleet became separated, with Quirós returning east to Mexico, and his navigator Torres travelling west through the straits between New Guinea and Australia that now bear his name (Beaglehole 1966: 92–104; Flexner et al. 2016: 210–14; Kelly 1966: 204–32; Markham 1904: 240–86, 371–95).

Sites associated with Mendaña's voyages were identified based on the presence of distinctive glazed Spanish pottery. Subsequent geochemical analyses showed the pottery included vessels produced in the Americas, primarily from Peru (Kelloway et al. 2013, 2014). Some of the pots brought by the Spanish were subsequently repurposed within indigenous Oceanic exchange networks, as sherds of Spanish *botijas* (olive jars) have also been found in Taumako, Solomon Islands, and Mota, Vanuatu, most likely associated with Quiros' 1605–1606 voyage (Bedford et al. 2009). Pottery exchange was a characteristic of indigenous inter-island trade in this part of the Pacific, though it might be speculated that the exotic vessels brought by bearded men in strange ships had particular values in these systems.

Other possible impacts of the early Spanish voyages include the likelihood that these first encounters with Old World infectious diseases had a negative impact on local populations. This is well documented in later encounters (e.g., Spriggs 2007) but more research would be needed to confirm this. In the long term, the primary influence of the sixteenth- and seventeenth-century Spanish navigators lies in the colonial toponymy that sits within the layers of place names in Vanuatu and the Solomon Islands (e.g., Jolly 2009).

During the seventeenth century, after declaring independence and forming a unified East India Company, the Dutch began sailing into the south seas via the Cape of Good Hope, navigating to, mapping, and occasionally crashing into the west coast of Australia (Beaglehole 1966: 108–37; Sheehan 2008). Eventually, Dutch navigators would enter the Pacific itself. The most significant Dutch voyage in the region was that led by Tasman from 1642 to 1643, who sailed with two ships, the *Heemskerck* and *Zeehaen*. Tasman followed the pattern of sailing into the Pacific from the west, but pushed further into the southwestern part of the grand ocean than any previous navigator. His voyage included the first European contacts with a large island that Tasman called 'Van Diemen's Land' after the governor-general of Batavia who sponsored the expedition (now Tasmania; Beaglehole 1966: 140–8). There is no record of direct contact with Aboriginal Tasmanians, though it is likely Tasman's ships and men were watched carefully from a safe distance.

Further east, Tasman's expedition reached the west coast of New Zealand, where he sailed north along the coast from near Punakaiki to Taitapu (Golden Bay). Here contact was brief and tragic. After their approach to shore was challenged by the local Māori and the Dutch responded with a show of firearms, Tasman decided to attempt an interaction while remaining on guard. A cockboat was launched from the *Heemskerck* to warn the sailors on the *Zeehaen* not to bring on too many visitors. As the cockboat was returning to its home ship, it was rammed by a Māori war canoe and the three sailors on board killed. The Dutch sent their pinnace with a contingent of heavily armed men to retrieve their compatriates. At this point a fleet of twenty-two canoes had arrived in the harbour. When half of the canoes approached the Dutch ships the European sailors sought revenge, killing at least one of the Māori, ironically a man alone in his canoe with a white flag, possibly a sign of contrition or call to treat (Salmond 1991: 71–84). Tasman's subsequent voyaging through Tonga, Fiji, and New Guinea likewise involved brief, if less violent, encounters (Beaglehole 1966: 152–6).

By the 1650s, Dutch enthusiasm for exploring the Pacific had waned. As Beaglehole (1966: 162) puts it, 'Anthony van Diemen died; Tasman sailed no more; the vision of a Dutch Pacific faded'. The remainder of the seventeenth and much of the eighteenth century was left to the emerging imperial powers, Great Britain and France, with some remnant Spanish influence. There were multiple global circumnavigations during the 1700s, including those by John Byron, Philip Carterer, Samuel Wallis, and Louis Antoine de Bougainville (Beaglehole 1966: 194–228).

Arguably the most prominent historical European navigator was James Cook, whose three voyages between 1768 and 1779 would transform the European understanding of the Pacific (Beaglehole 1966: 229–315). Like previous navigators, Cook of course didn't sail alone or without the leading technology of his day. In addition to advances in sailing technology, Cook benefitted from the invention of precision chronometers that allowed for reliable marking of longitude, something that had been practically impossible before the 1760s (Sobel 1995). One could fill a small library with biographies and historical accounts (e.g., Salmond 2003; Sahlins 1995), transcriptions of Cook's own diaries (Beaglehole 1955, 1967, 1969), as well as related archives, ephemera, and artefacts such as Islander objects collected by Johann and Reinhold Forster, the expedition's resident scientists (Coote et al. 2000).

Because Cook's history and legacy are so massive, I will focus on episodes from each of the three monumental expeditions that are illustrative of the history of these encounters, and the experiences of Pacific Islanders in the last decades of the time when the Pacific remained largely uncolonised. Cook's first voyage to the Pacific was undertaken ostensibly to observe the 1769 Transit of Venus from a tropical latitude, but he also had secret orders to further explore and even claim territories for the British Crown (Beaglehole 1966: 233–4; Maor 2004: 99–105). It is no small irony that, while Cook generally left the Pacific Islanders he encountered to maintain their own sovereignty, he somewhat uncharacteristically claimed the entire Australian landmass for the Crown after sailing along the east coast in 1770, opening the way for the eventual British colonisation of that continent (Schlunke 2007).

In July 1769, following the observation of the Transit and establishing relationships with the Tahitian *'arioi* (an aristocratic class who were specialists in dance, song, and sacred forms of entertainment), the *Endeavour* departed from Tahiti. On board was a priest and master navigator called Tupaia. The British believed that Tupaia would prove useful because of his status in Tahitian society, and more importantly because he appeared to have great knowledge of the other islands in the area. Tupaia, for his part, was not on board as a neutral guide or observer. Tupaia's home island in the Windward Islands, Ra'iatea, had been invaded some years ago by warriors from Borabora. Tupaia was convinced that Cook and his red-coated Marines (*'ura*, red, being a sacred colour associated with power and authority) with their firearms would be able to defeat the invaders from Borarbora and restore the proper chiefly lineage to power in Ra'iatea (Salmond 2009: 203–4).

Sailing to the west, Tupaia was 'taking Cook, Banks, Solander and their shipmates on an *"arioi* voyage' through the Leeward Islands (Salmond 2009: 207). The goal of the journey was to solidify the alliance with the British in order to cast out the hated Boraborans. During his time aboard the *Endeavour*, Tupaia learned sketching and watercolours from the British. While sailing west, Tupaia demonstrated his great geographical knowledge, naming 130 islands and how to sail to them, as well as producing both a chart of the Leeward Islands and a remarkable chart of seventy-four islands in surrounding groups (Dorbe-Larcade and Tumuhai 2019: 88). Tupaia's Chart, as the latter document is called, was co-constructed with Cook and based on the immense voyaging knowledge Tupaia had learned as a student of the school of master navigators at Taputapuatea, one of the most sacred sites in the Society Islands (Salmond 2009: 204, 221–2).

The chart includes islands scattered over 3,500 kilometers of ocean from east to west. The Tahitian master navigator had himself sailed as far away as islands in Tonga and the Australs. Tupaia's chart is not, strictly speaking, 'accurate' in a Western cartographic sense. Rather, it contains a mixture of European conventions and Pacific Islander understandings of navigation between islands. A recent re-analysis of the chart shows that when it is understood that different islands are placed in terms of their relative position, it can be understood as 'a mosaic of subject-centred sailing directions or bearings to distant islands' (Di Piazza and Pearthree 2007: 324). Tupaia was attempting to translate information that was given to him via oral traditions for Cook in a format that he thought a fellow navigator from over the horizon would be able to understand.

After a voyage of several days, Tupaia and the crew of the *Endeavour* arrived in Huahine. Here too people were anxious about the increasingly bellicose warriors from Borabora. Tupaia had several estates on this island, which was also the location of Taputapuatea where he was trained in navigation and various other sacred arts and rituals. Meeting the paramount chief of Huahine, Ori, Cook still refused to commit to attacking the Boraborans. But, as they were departing Ra'iatea, Cook raised the English Jack, proclaiming the Leeward Islands for King George III (a claim the Crown ultimately did not really pursue beyond sending a few missionaries later in the 1800s). Through this act, the British fulfilled a prophecy in which a canoe without an outrigger carrying a new kind of people would arrive to take over the islands (though there may be some reason to doubt the veracity of this prophecy, at least in the ways it is usually represented in British historiography; see Dorbe-Larcade and Tumahai 2019: 76–7). As Salmond (2009: 210) puts it, 'Escorted by their red-coated warriors (the marines), the strangers had just proclaimed the *mana* of their gods over Taputapuatea, the most sacred site in the Society Islands.'

The *'arioi* journey continued. Banks broke a major *tabu* by not only touching but damaging the extremely sacred wrapped image of the god 'Oro at Taputapuatea. Cook nearly wrecked the *Endeavour* on the reef when he ignored Tupaia's instructions and tried to sail through the *noa* (profane) pass from 'Opoa harbour rather than the *ra'a* (sacred) one. Nonetheless the British continued to be entertained by the sketches, dances, and stories of their *'arioi* hosts. Cook never did attack Borabora, and the British were unimpressed with the Boraboran warrior chief Puni who they encountered occupying Tupaia's birth-place of Ha'amanino Bay, Ra'iatea. After making sure the ship was well-stocked with provisions, the *Endeavour* departed the Society Islands and, to Tupaia's dismay, turned not west as he had suggested, but south (Salmond 2009: 211–19).

In October 1769, the *Endeavour* sighted land. The landmass was larger than any the crew had seen. It was thought that the *Endeavour* had finally encoun-tered *Terra Australis*, but subsequently the navigators realised they had simply re-discovered the islands of New Zealand, which Tasman had visited over 120 years earlier. More surprisingly, Tupaia found he could understand the local language and served as translator for the expedition, even though he had no previous knowledge of any islands this far south. Despite this linguistic advan-tage, Cook's expedition was only slightly more successful in establishing relationships with Māori people and there were several violent encounters. Tupaia, however, was welcomed as a *tohunga* (expert or priest) from the ancestral homeland of *Hawaiki*. Sadly little was recorded of his interactions with Māori chiefs and priests, but this reconnection of Tahiti and Aotearoa generations after the original fleet of *waka* arrived must have inspired quite unprecedented conversations (Salmond 2009: 225–32; for a more detailed account see Salmond 1991: 119–296). Leaving New Zealand, Cook made west and north, eventually encountering the coast of Australia. Tupaia con-tinued on the *Endeavour* to Batavia, where he eventually became ill and died (Salmond 2009: 233–5). Tupaia ended up far indeed from his Society Islands homeland but left a unique legacy among Polynesian master navigators through his journeys on the *Endeavour*.

On his second journey in the Pacific, Cook, now with two ships, *Resolution* and *Adventure*, sailed through the islands of what is now Vanuatu from north to south in July–August 1774. The ships spent several days in Malakula, where Cook offered a gift of a pair of dogs from the Society Islands to the local people (Beaglehole 1969: 460–8). Continuing south, Cook attempted a landing to gather wood and water on the island now called Erromango, because as the

Islanders saw the British approaching the shore, they brought an offering of yams, shouting, '*Armae, ngo!*' ('it is good to eat'; Huffman 1996: 129). It is likely that the strange ships and stranger-looking people were identified as *natemas* (spirits), and it was thought that a propitiatory offering of food would see them off before they caused harm. But there seems to have been some confusion over what was happening and how to react, among both the Erromangans and the British. A man Cook identified as a chief tried to board the boat that had rowed to the shore, while others tried to seize the boat and its oars. Panicking, Cook ordered his crew to fire on the assembled crowd and the British retreated under a hail of stones and arrows from the shore (Beaglehole 1969: 477–80).

Sailing south again, that night Cook was excited to notice a red glow and thunderous noise indicative of a live volcano. As before, Cook's expedition had a dual purpose, both to chart and where appropriate claim new territories for the British Crown, and to advance scientific knowledge. A previously unknown volcano would make a wonderful discovery to report upon returning home. *Resolution* and *Adventure* sailed the next day into a wide, calm harbour which Cook named for the former ship. Again the ships were met with curious local people, who sailed and paddled out in their canoes, only to be scattered through the use of firearms. This time Cook's crew shot without intent to harm, and an old man, Paowang, made several trips to the ships to exchange yams and coconuts for whatever the crew would give him (Beaglehole 1969: 480–3). This was the island of Tanna, another misnomer caused by Forster taking the words used when he pointed to the ground for the name of the island ('*ta na*' literally means 'ground' or 'earth' in the Tannese languages; Jolly 2009: 85).

The next day, Cook and crew went ashore for fresh water, and were met with a crowd Cook estimated at over 1,000 people divided into two groups (possibly the two groups represented the 'moieties' of *Kaviameta* and *Numrukuen*; see Bonnemaison 1994: 148–53). On the shore, there was a bundle of food including a yam, two taro roots, and plantains (bananas). Significantly, the food was marked with 'four small reeds about two feet from each other in a line at right angles to the sea shore' (Beaglehole 1969: 484). These were almost certainly *tabu* markers meant to determine whether the new arrivals were *ierehma* (spirits; see Flexner et al. 2018b: 258). As they gathered water and made some minor exchanges of cloth and beads for coconuts and yams, the crew were again reduced to using firearms to disperse the crowds (Beaglehole 1969: 483–6).

The British sailors were eventually able to establish friendly relationships. They remained wary of the fact that the Tannese men went about with clubs and bows, which they would display menacingly when challenged, though none of the British were ever attacked during the encounter. Cook befriended a local chief called Wha-a-gou and the old man, Paowang, with whom he exchanged gifts. Cook made geological observations, and Forster was able to collect botanical specimens and some 'curios' from the local people despite initial resistance to trade (Beaglehole 1969: 491–8). Their attempts to get close to the volcano, Iasur, however, were stymied and expeditions inland were often turned back, with the explorers finding themselves returned to the beach by local 'guides'. Iasur is a sacred space and ancestral being, and it is likely the Tannese believed it was too risky to expose such an important inspirited place to the unpredictable visitors (Flexner et al. 2018b: 259).

As was seemingly inevitable in these kinds of encounters, the friendly relationships built over a course of days were shattered with violence. The ship's sentry, William Wedgeborough, fired upon a Tannese man, in an attack that Cook described as unprovoked and unjustified (Beaglehole 1969: 499). The next morning, the *Resolution* and *Endeavour* summarily departed, sailing over the horizon again. As the encounter passed from history, to memory, to myth, the Tannese shifted the story to one that represented their control over European foreigners. In recounting their memory of Cook's visit to missionary George Turner in the 1840s, Tannese people suggested that a powerful *tupunas* (sorcerer) had summoned the two British ships to settle a local dispute by attacking a rival magic user, after which the British departed (Adams 1984: 31). Thus the magical efficacy of the Tannese replaced European agency in the encounter.

Like Magellan 260 years before him, Cook would not return from his third and final voyage. The sequence of events leading to Cook's death have been written and rewritten in various formats since the time of their happening, including in one of the more spirited and extensive anthropological debates of the 1990s (Obeyesekere 1992; Sahlins 1985: 104–35; Sahlins 1995). The basic historical facts of who, when, and where are generally understood. In January 1778, Cook first sighted Kaua'i, in the northwest of the main Hawaiian Islands (a small island, Ni'ihau lies to the west, and two additional high islands and a number of coral atolls continue the northwestern Hawaiian chain across a distance of over 2,500 km). This was the first time Europeans had visited the geographically isolated archipelago. The crew of Cook's ships for this voyage, the *Resolution* and *Discovery*, spent four days trading successfully and replenishing provisions before returning to a northward course in searching for a 'Northwest Passage' that theoretically would offer speedier and thus more profitable trade between Europe and Asia (Beaglehole 1966: 296–7; Kuykendall 1965: 12–14).

In late November, Cook returned to the Hawaiian Islands, this time sighting, but not landing on, the island of Maui because he thought trade with the islanders was better regulated from over the bows of his ship. In December the island of Hawai'i, largest and southeasternmost in the group, was sighted. Again Cook chose to coast rather than land, though after being caught in a storm he finally decided that the *Resolution* and *Discovery* needed to rest and refit. He landed in Kealakekua Bay, intending to do so on 17 January 1779 (Beaglehole 1966: 301–2; Kuykendall 1965: 16). It was in Kealakekua that Cook became unwittingly entangled in the events that would lead to his death.

Cook was pleased to find he was honoured in a way he had never experienced in all his time in Polynesia. He was greeted by thousands of canoes filled with people chanting and singing, which were filled with produce, pigs, and fish that were freely offered to the British sailors. Further, the crowd carried no weapon and made no sign of threat. The priests took Cook to the local *heiau* (temple), where he was dressed in sacred red *kapa* (barkcloth). His ships were well provisioned, with daily offerings of pigs and baked root vegetables. A friendly exchange was taken up, and gifts of iron adzes and daggers were made. The *ali'i nui* of the area, Kalani'ōpu'u, dressed Cook in his feather cape and helmet, a high honour indeed. All seemed to be going well from the British perspective. On 4 February, the *Resolution* and *Discovery* departed early in the morning, sailing to the north, but they encountered a strong wind that snapped the foremast of the *Resolution* (Beaglehole 1966: 302–4; Kuykendall 1965: 16–17).

They returned to Kealakekua for repairs on 11 February, but did not find the warm welcome they had previously enjoyed. Thefts targeted increasingly valuable property on the British ships, culminating in the disappearance of the cutter from the *Discovery*. Cook intervened, determined to take Kalani'ōpu'u hostage to force the cutter's return. Kalani'ōpu'u, despite initially appearing compliant, eventually declined. In a twist of fate, and unknown to Cook, another local chief had been shot by the British while attempting to escape the British blockade of the harbour. There was an altercation on the beach as Cook attempted to return to his ship. The great British navigator was stabbed several times by the very daggers he and his men had given as gifts, and his body was taken to the same *heiau* where he had been given the highest imaginable honours less than a month prior (Beaglehole 1966: 304–6; Kuykendall 1965: 18–20).

Historical anthropologist Marshall Sahlins (1985: 104–35; 1995) explains Cook's death in Hawaiian terms. Kealakekua literally translates as 'the path of the god'. It is the location on Hawai'i Island where the annual Makahiki rituals begin and end. Makahiki is a period marked by the rising and setting of the constellation Pleiades between January and February, precisely when the *Resolution* and *Discovery* began their journey around Maui and Hawai'i.

Cook, coming from the northwest, followed the path of the Hawaiian god Lono, to whom the Makahiki period is dedicated. The white sails of the British ships matched Lono's insignia, a cross-piece from which are hung white *kapa* cloth and the skin of the *ka'upu* bird. Thus it was not a great difficulty for the Hawaiians, seeing strange, massive ships hung with square rigging and white sails, coming from the right direction at the right time, as a portent of Lono's arrival. It was not much of an additional leap to identify Cook, clearly the leader of this floating chiefdom, as Lono himself (Sahlins 1985: 115–18).

Makahiki coincides with the rainy season in Hawai'i. It is a period of peace, feasting, *communitas*, and relaxation of *kapu* (ritual restrictions). At the end of Makahiki, Lono is sacrificed and the war god, Kū, restored to power and ritual prominence. Sahlins (1985: 128–31) identifies the crisis Cook and Kalani'ōpu'u faced in terms of a sacred politics. The restoration of Kū and the order of *kapu* was critical to the authority of Hawaiian kings. Thus when Cook-as-Lono departs at the end of Makahiki, all is well. Except, Cook departed by the wrong route, as sea-going Makahiki circuits are made with the island to the left of the vessel. When Cook then returned to Kealakekua, the order of things was in threat with both immediate political and more sacred, universal, implications.

Cook's presence in Kealakekua created a 'mythopolitical crisis' (Sahlins 1985: 127). As Sahlins (1985: 104–35; 1995) argues, the structure of this situation makes Cook's death almost necessary or inevitable (though see the counter-argument in Obeyesekere 1992). The Hawaiians could only understand through their own worldview (Sahlins 1995), and the 'arguments' offered by Cook and his officers about their need to return were moot, beyond reason. Order and control were lost and Lono was sacrificed, as must happen at that point in the mythical structure. Yet even after Cook's death and before the departure of the British sailors, the Lono priests continued sending supplies and gifts. There are hints of expectation for Lono to return in similar fashion in subsequent years, even among those who had seen Cook die on the beach in Kealakekua (Sahlins 1985: 125–6).

As Beaglehole (1966: 316) concludes his account of this era, 'When the *Resolution* and *Discovery* returned from that last four years' voyage they returned from an ocean known thenceforth in all its main features ... In place of the continent [*Terra Australis Incognita*] that was no more than a shadow of the mind, were islands almost beyond computation, and in 1780 there were few archipelagos of importance that had escaped discovery and identification. In essentials the modern map had assumed its form.' There were still explorers after Cook (see Rigby et al. 2005), including Vasily Mikhailovich Golovnin (Russian), George Vancouver (British), and Jules Sébastien César Dumont

D'Urville (French). Prodigious feats of navigation also continued, such as those of William Bligh, particularly following the infamous *Bounty* mutiny (Dening 1992; Salmond 2011). Nor was Cook the last navigator to lose his life because of entanglement in a cultural landscape he didn't understand, as demonstrated in the death of the Cambridge scholar William Gooch in Hawai'i (Dening 1988). However, it could be argued that the era of 'heroic' voyaging in the Pacific was coming to an end. By the early 1800s, almost all of the islands in Oceania had been charted, and many had been claimed by European powers as part of growing empires.

Dening (1980, 2004) uses the graceful metaphor of 'the beach' to represent the symbolic and actual place where many moments of contact happened between Europeans and Pacific Islanders. For the people on the other side of the encounter this period, which indeed resulted in countless European 'discoveries', was also a time when Oceanic peoples became aware of a wider world beyond their vast saltwater estate. Yet Islanders still held the upper hand in most interactions, and had already begun finding ways to entangle and leverage the foreign interlopers within their own affairs. While European powers would become more interventionist in the next centuries, those who came from the island side of the beach would find ways to shape these interactions according to their own desires, political struggles, and cosmologies.

7 From a Millennium of Contacts to Islander Futures

While this Element is primarily a history, it should be noted that for many Pacific Islanders, their history is experienced as a living one (e.g., Martinsson-Wallin 2011). Many of the UNESCO World Heritage Sites in the Pacific, including Kuk Swamp (Papua New Guinea), Nan Madol (Pohnpei), Roi Mata's Domain (Vanuatu), and Taputapuatea (Tahiti), use criterion vi: 'to be directly or tangibly associated with events or living traditions, with ideas, or with beliefs, with artistic and literary works of outstanding universal significance' (UNESCO 2019: 26; see also Smith 2007). Ballard (2014) describes the presence of the past in lived experience for Oceanic peoples and their interlocutors in terms of 'historicities'. Historicities go beyond history as typically understood by including those elements of the past that exist in the present and future, are sensual and performative, and in some ways remain inscrutable because they involve explanations that derive from beyond the physical world. Pacific histories are a key for unlocking a decolonised future in the region (see Banivanua Mar 2016).

In the languages of Tanna Island, people use the same words to describe the deep past and the far future (in the Nafé language of the southeast of the island, the term is *kwumweisin*; Lindstrom 2011: 146). It would be tempting to see this as a stereotypical case of indigenous temporalities as 'cyclical' as opposed to 'linear' Western understandings of time, but I would propose something more expansive (see also Dening 2004). When Christian missionaries arrived in Tanna and began looking for a word to closely translate as 'God', they settled on *Kwumweisin* (or *Uhngen* in the other languages of the island; see Gray 1892: 21–2). I would suggest it means something closer to 'infinity'. In other words, no, the Tannese probably do not understand their history in a straight line, though they are capable of seeing historical events in such a way. There are known historical ruptures, such as when Tannese ancestors became Christians, or when Mwatiktiki brought pigs and 'real' kava to the island where earlier people had eaten rats and drunk wild kava. But a Tannese historicity based in *kwumweisin* expands outwards in all directions, all at once. There is no ultimate rupture between past, present, and future, so the telling of those pasts represents an invocation of what happens in all times.

In drawing this Element to a close, I want to turn to what the historicity of a millennium of cross-cultural interactions in Oceania might mean for Islander presents and futures. Working in the Pacific Northwest of North America, Gonzalez et al. (2018) see historical archaeology as a critical element of expanding horizons for indigenous peoples looking ahead. Schmidt and Pikirayi (2018) are more pessimistic when discussing the state of the field in Africa and its failure to engage meaningfully with problems relevant to the local people. In the Pacific, articulations of the value of archaeology for living communities while also acknowledging its problematic colonial past are increasingly articulated by Islanders themselves (e.g., Kawelu and Pakele 2014; O'Regan 2016). As my colleague from the Vanuatu Cultural Centre Edson Willie (2019: 211) puts it, 'being an archaeologist and a ni-Vanuatu has allowed me to attune the custom beliefs and practices of local communities with archaeological practices. Seeing the two sides of the same coin brings a sense of security and peace to the community, which then becomes a fertile ground for harmonious working relationships with archaeologists.'

This is not to say there is no conflict or dissent in Vanuatu or Pacific archaeology by any means. We have much work to do before we have a truly egalitarian Pacific archaeology, anthropology, or history. There are simply too many unresolved contradictions stemming from the colonial past in the present (Flexner 2018). But the relationships we build and the stories we share can and often do contribute to the historicities of the Pacific Islands, often in ways that are not predictable or controllable. Oceanic people face a number of contemporary challenges, from climate change, to maintaining control over and managing resources on land and at sea, to finding pathways to greater autonomy and self-direction in a still-colonised world, to conserving languages and customs. The Oceanic past is critical to understanding all of these things in the present and future. Oceanic historicities are brought to life through stories told over a campfire, in art, dance, and music, and, sometimes, in works of academic literature.

It would be conceited indeed to suggest that works such as this, of the Western tradition, deriving from Western institutions, and meant largely for Western audiences, are 'Oceanic' in nature, particularly as my own ancestors lie in other parts of the world. What I would suggest instead is that this Element offers to the reader a chance to consider the historicities that emerge from a millennium during which Polynesian navigators reached the ends of the Pacific, encountering new lands and in some cases new people; a time during which the region's great indigenous political sagas played out; and a period when Europeans and other interlopers were encountered but had yet to affect major changes to the scenery in terms of demography, environment, political economy, and religion. Yet throughout periods of historical change and continuity, Pacific Islanders have remained adaptive and resilient. They have continued to orate, dance, sing, and increasingly write, their own stories on their terms. Customs and traditions continue to be passed on, many of which derive from ancestral beings, both human and non-human, and their respective historicities.

I will leave the final word to two Vanuatu Cultural Centre fieldworkers and mentors of mine. The late Jerry Taki is from Erromango Island, and wrote about the importance of his work in both his native Syé language and English (quoted in Naupa 2011: 128).

> *Yacamentavsogi ovoteme omwisu magkau Erromango gi nompi, momporipmi im nam enogkoh. Ire, yamentavsogi ovonyan gin am enogkoh im woretai gin am enogkoh. Tavniri enyau, kolentavsogi ovonyan enogkoh gi nelcavi domo nompi nomporipmi im nam enogkoh amurep dan su.*

'I teach Erromangans about our custom and culture and language. Today, I also teach children to speak and write Syé and how to make *tapa*. In my opinion, we must continue to teach our children our custom, culture and language so that it will not be lost.'

Takaronga Kuautonga, *man Futuna*, co-translated a traditional song with anthropologist Janet Keller playfully describing the mission encounter on his island in terms of the lobster trap (*nahjeiji*). The final verse, focusing on revival and return to traditional places of knowledge, seems particularly appropriate to close with (Keller and Kuautonga 2007: 254–5):

> *'Kautaina ta vaka oku*
> *Makaafe i ahe rotumai sau Ritoga.'*
> *'Reijikijia Mis(t)i Limpia, rofano uauta*

Rofijikake i Weia kai nimeiinu i a Namtamorou'
(Alternatively Namtanarau/Namtamataga)

'We will fill my canoe
And return with the south wind.'
'When the wind makes white caps
at Mis(t)i Limpia, then
we'll go shoreward
To ascend to Weia and drink
from Namtamorou
(a spring and local source of knowledge)'

References

Adams, R. (1984). *In the Land of Strangers: A Century of European Contact with Tanna, 1774–1874*, Canberra: Australian National University Press.

Allen, J. & R. C. Green (1972). Mendana 1595 and the Fate of the Lost 'Almiranta': An Archaeological Investigation. *Journal of Pacific History*, 7, 73–91.

Anderson, A. (2002). A Fragile Plenty: Pre-European Maori and the New Zealand Environment, in *Environmental Histories of New Zealand*, eds. E. Pawson & T. Brooking, Auckland: Oxford University Press, 19–34.

Anderson, A. (2006). Polynesian Seafaring and American Horizons: A Response to Jones and Klar. *American Antiquity*, 71(4), 759–64.

Anderson, A. (2009). Prehistoric Archaeology in the Auckland Islands, New Zealand Subarctic Region, in *Care of the Southern Ocean: An Archaeological and Historical Survey of the Auckland Islands*, eds. P. R. Dingwall, K. L. Jones, & R. Egerton, Auckland: New Zealand Archaeological Association, 9–38.

Anderson, A., J. Binney, & A. Harris (2014). *Tangata Whenua: An Illustrated History*, Wellington: Bridget Williams Books.

Anderson, A. & D. J. Kennett (eds.) (2012). *Taking the High Ground: The Archaeology of Rapa, a Fortified Island in Remote East Polynesia*, Canberra: Australian National University Press.

Arnold, J. E. (2007). Credit Where Credit is Due: The History of the Chumash Oceangoing Plank Canoes. *American Antiquity*, 72(2), 196–209.

Athens, J. S. (2009). *Rattus exulans* and the Catastrophic Disappearance of Hawai'i's Native Lowland Forest. *Biological Invasions*, 11(7), 1489–501.

Athens, J. S. (2011). *Latte* Period Occupation on Pagan and Sarigan, Northern Mariana Islands. *Journal of Island and Coastal Archaeology*, 6(2), 314–330.

Athens, J. S., T. M. Rieth, & T. S. Dye (2014). A Paleoenvironmental and Archaeological Model-Based Age Estimate for the Colonization of Hawaii. *American Antiquity*, 79(1), 144–55.

Bairnes, S. E. (forthcoming). *The Global Middle Ages: Cahokia and the North American World*, Cambridge: Cambridge University Press Elements Series in the Global Middle Ages.

Ballard, C. (2014). Oceanic Historicities. *The Contemporary Pacific*, 26(1), 96–124.

Ballard, C. (2016). The Legendary Roi Mata. *Connexions*, 4, 98–111.

Ballard, C. (2020). The Lizard in the Volcano: Narratives of the Kuwae Eruption. *The Contemporary Pacific*, 32(1), 98–123.

Banivanua Mar, T. (2016). *Decolonisation and the Pacific: Indigenous Globalisation and the Ends of Empire*, Cambridge: Cambridge University Press.

Bayliss-Smith, T., M. Prebble, & S. Manebosa (2019). Saltwater and Bush in New Georgia, Solomon Islands: Exchange Relations, Agricultural Intensification and Limits to Social Complexity, in *Archaeologies of Island Melanesia: Current Approaches to Landscapes, Exchange, and Practice*, eds. M. Leclerc & J. L. Flexner, Canberra: Australian National University Press, 35–52.

Beaglehole, J. C. (ed.) (1955). *The Journals of Captain James Cook, Volume 1*, Cambridge: The Hakluyt Society.

Beaglehole, J. C. (1966). *The Exploration of the Pacific*, Palo Alto, CA: Stanford University Press.

Beaglehole, J. C. (ed.) (1967). *The Journals of Captain James Cook on his Voyages of Discovery: Voyage of the Resolution and Discovery 1776–1780, Part One*, Cambridge: The Hakluyt Society.

Beaglehole, J. C. (ed.) (1969). *The Journals of Captain James Cook on His Voyages of Discovery: The Voyage of the Resolution and Adventure 1772–1775*, Cambridge: The Hakluyt Society.

Beck, W. & M. Somerville (2005). Conversations between Disciplines: Historical Archaeology and Oral History at Yarrawarra. *World Archaeology*, 37(3), 468–83.

Bedford, S. (2006). *Pieces of the Vanuatu Puzzle: Archaeology of the North, South, and Centre*, Canberra: Australian National University Press.

Bedford, S. (2013). From Paeroa to Pohue Pa: Remnant Landscapes of Events that Once Shook the World, in *Finding our Recent Past: Historical Archaeology in New Zealand*, eds. M. Campbell, S. Holdaway, & S. Macready, Auckland: New Zealand Archaeological Association, 59–76.

Bedford, S. (2019). The Complexity of Monumentality in Melanesia: Mixed Messages from Vanuatu, in *Archaeologies of Island Melanesia: Current Approaches to Landscapes, Exchange, and Practice*, eds. M. Leclerc & J. L. Flexner, Canberra: Australian National University Press, 67–80.

Bedford, S., W. R. Dickinson, R. C. Green, & G. K. Ward (2009). Detritus of Empire: Seventeenth Century Spanish Pottery from Taumako, Southeast Solomon Islands, and Mota, Northern Vanuatu. *Journal of the Polynesian Society*, 118(1), 69–90.

Bonnemaison, J. (1994). *The Tree and the Canoe: History and Ethnogeography of Tanna*, Honolulu, HI: University of Hawaii Press.

Burley, D. V. (2013). Fijian Polygenesis and the Melanesia/Polynesia Divide. *Current Anthropology*, 54(4), 436–62.

Burley, D. V., T. Freeland, & J. Balenaivalu (2016). Nineteenth-Century Conflict and the Koivuanabuli Fortification Complex on Mali Island, Northern Fiji. *Journal of Island and Coastal Archaeology*, 11(1), 107–21.

Burley, D. V., M. I. Weisler, & J.-x. Zhao (2012). High Precision U/Th Dating of First Polynesian Settlement. *PLoS-One*, 7(11), 1–6.

Campbell, M. (2008). The Historical Archaeology of New Zealand's Prehistory, in *Islands of Inquiry: Colonisation, Seafaring and the Archaeology of Maritime Landscapes*, eds. G. Clark, F. Leach, & S. O'Connor, Canberra: Australian National University Press, 339–50.

Carson, M. T. (2012). Recent Developments in Prehistory. Perspectives on Settlement Chronology, Inter-Community Relations, and Identity Formation, in *Polynesian Outliers: The State of the Art*, eds. R. Feinberg & R. Scaglion, Pittsburgh, PA: University of Pittsburgh Press, 27–48.

Clark, G. (2003). Dumont d'Urville's Oceania. *Journal of Pacific History*, 38 (2), 155–61.

Clark, G., D. V. Burley, & T. Murray (2008). Monumentality and the Development of the Tongan Maritime Chiefdom. *Antiquity*, 82(318), 994–1008.

Clark, G. R., C. Reepmeyer, N. Melekiola, W. R. Dickinson, & H. Martinsson-Wallin (2014). Stone Tools from the Ancient Tongan State Reveal Prehistoric Interaction Centers in the Central Pacific. *Proceedings of the National Academy of Sciences*, 111(29), 10491–6.

Clarke, A. C., M. K. Burtenshaw, P. A. McLenachan, D. L. Erickson, & D. Penny (2006). Reconstructing the Origins and Dispersal of the Polynesian Bottle Gourd (*Lagenaria siceraria*). *Molecular Biology and Evolution*, 23(5), 893–900.

Clarkson, C., Z. Jacobs, B. Marwick, R. Fullagar, L. Wallis, M. Smith, R. G. Roberts, E. Hayes, K. Lowe, X. Carah, S. A. Florin, J. McNeil, D. Cox, L. J. Arnold, Q. Hua, J. Huntley, H. E. A. Brand, T. Manne, A. Fairbairn, J. Shulmeister, L. Lyle, M. Salinas, M. Page, K. Connell, G. Park, K. Norman, T. Murphy, & C. Pardoe (2017). Human Occupation of Northern Australia by 65000 Years Ago. *Nature*, 547, 306–10.

Cochrane, E. E. (2021). Pacific Island Archaeology and Evolutionary Theory, in *Theory in the Pacific, the Pacific in Theory: Archaeological Perspectives*, ed. T. Thomas, London: Routledge, 58–78.

Collerson, K. D. & M. I. Weisler (2007). Stone Adze Compositions and the Extent of Ancient Polynesian Voyaging and Trade. *Science*, 317(5846), 1907–11.

Comer, D. C., J. A. Comer, I. A. Dumitru, W. S. Ayres, M. J. Levin, K. A. Seikel, D. A. White, & M. J. Harrower (2019). Airborne LiDAR Reveals a Vast Archaeological Landscape at the Nan Madol World Heritage Site. *Remote Sensing*, 11(2152), 1–24.

Conte, E. & P. V. Kirch. (2004). *Archaeological Investigations in the Mangareva Islands (Gambier Archipelago), French Polynesia*, Berkeley, CA: University of California, Berkeley Archaeological Research Facility.

Coote, J., P. Gathercole, N. Meister, T. Rogers, & F. Midgley (2000). 'Curiosities Sent to Oxford': The Original Documentation of the Forster Collection at the Pitt Rivers Museum. *Journal of the History of Collections*, 12(2), 177–92.

Craib, J. L. (1986). Casas de los Antiguos: Social Differentiation in Protohistoric Chamorro Society, Marianas Islands. Unpublished PhD dissertation, University of Sydney.

Crowley, T. (2000). The Language Situation in Vanuatu. *Current Issues in Language Planning*, 1(1), 47–132.

David, B., L. Lamb, J.-J. Delannoy, F. Pivoru, C. Rowe, M. Pivoru, T. Frank, N. Frank, A. Fairbairn, & R. Pivoru (2012). Poromoi Tamu and the Case of the Drowning Village: History, Lost Places and the Stories We Tell. *International Journal of Historical Archaeology*, 16(2), 319–45.

Dening, G. (1980). *Islands and Beaches: Discourse on a Silent Land, Marquesas, 1774–1880*, Melbourne: Melbourne University Press.

Dening, G. (1988). *History's Anthropology: The Death of William Gooch*, Lanham, MD: University Press of America.

Dening, G. (1992). *Mr. Bligh's Bad Language: Passion, Power and Theatre on the Bounty*, Cambridge: Cambridge University Press.

Dening, G. (2004). *Beach Crossings: Voyaging Across Times, Cultures, and Self*, Philadelphia, PA: University of Pennsylvania Press.

Di Piazza, A. & E. Pearthree (2007). A New Reading of Tupaia's Chart. *Journal of the Polynesian Society*, 116(3), 321–40.

Diamond, J. (2005). *Collapse: How Societies Choose to Fail or Succeed*, New York: Viking.

Doran, E. (1981). *Wangka: Austronesian Canoe Origins*, College Station, TX: Texas A&M University Press.

Dorbe-Lacarde, V. & L. Tumuhai (2019). Histoire des premiers contacts avec l'Occident (1767–1797), in *Une Histoire de Tahiti des Origines à Nos Jours*, ed. E. Conte Pape'ete: Au Vent Des Îles, 73–116.

Douglas, B. (1996). *Across the Great Divide: Journeys in History and Anthropology*, Amsterdam: Harwood Academic Press.

Dye, T. S. (1989). Tales of Two Cultures: Traditional Historical and Archaeological Interpretations of Hawaiian Prehistory. *B.P. Bishop Museum Occasional Papers*, 29, 3–22.

Dye, T. S. (2010). Social Transformation in Old Hawai'i: A Bottom-Up Approach. *American Antiquity*, 75(4), 727–42.

Dye, T. S. (2015). Dating Human Dispersal in Remote Oceania: A Bayesian View from Hawai'i. *World Archaeology*, 47(4), 661–76.

Earle, T. K. (1978). *Economic and Social Organization of a Complex Chiefdom: The Halelea District, Kaua'i, Hawaii*, Ann Arbor, MI: Museum of Anthropology, University of Michigan.

Fabian, J. (1983). *Time and the Other: How Anthropology Makes its Object*, New York: Columbia University Press.

Fairbairn, A., G. Hope, & G. Summerhayes (2017). Pleistocene Occupation of New Guinea's Highland and Subalpine Environments. *World Archaeology*, 38(3), 371–86.

Feinberg, R. & R. Scaglion (eds.) (2012). *Polynesian Outliers: The State of the Art*, Pittsburgh, PA: University of Pittsburgh Press.

Field, J. S. (1998). Natural and Constructed Defenses in Fijian Fortifications. *Asian Perspectives*, 37(1), 32–58.

Field, J. S., P. V. Kirch, K. L. Kawelu, & T. N. Ladefoged (2010). Households and Hierarchy: Domestic Modes of Production in Leeward Kohala, Hawai'i Island. *The Journal of Island and Coastal Archaeology*, 5(1), 52–85.

Finney, B. R. (1979). *Hokule'a: The Way to Tahiti*, New York: Dodd, Mead and Co.

Firth, R. (1961). *History and Traditions of Tikopia*, Wellington: The Polynesian Society.

Fischer, S. R. (1997). *Rongorongo, the Easter Island Script: History, Traditions, Texts*, Oxford: Oxford University Press.

Fitzpatrick, S. (2003). Stones of the Butterfly: An Archaeological Investigation of Yapese Stone Money Quarries in Palau, Western Caroline Islands, Micronesia. PhD thesis, University of Oregon.

Fitzpatrick, S. & McKeon, S. (2019). Banking on Stone Money: Ancient Antecedents to Bitcoin. *Economic Anthropology*, 7(1), 7–21.

Fleisher, J., P. Lane, A. LaViolette, M. Horton, E. Pollard, E. Quintana Morales, T. Vernet, A. Christie, & S. Wynne-Jones (2015). When Did the Swahili Become Maritime? *American Anthropologist*, 117(1), 100–15.

Flexner, J. L. (2014a). Historical Archaeology, Contact, and Colonialism in Oceania. *Journal of Archaeological Research*, 22(1), 43–87.

Flexner, J. L. (2014b). Mapping Local Perspectives in the Historical Archaeology of Vanuatu Mission Landscapes. *Asian Perspectives*, 53(1), 2–28.

Flexner, J. L. (2018). Doing Archaeology in Non-State Space. *Journal of Contemporary Archaeology*, 5(2), 254–9.

Flexner, J. L. (2020). Oceania, in *The Routledge Handbook of Global Historical Archaeology*, eds. C. E. Orser, A. Zarankin, P. P. Funari, S. Lawrence, & J. Symonds, London: Routledge, 712–30.

Flexner, J. L. (2021). Anarchist Theory in the Pacific and 'Pacific Anarchists' in Archaeological Thought, in *Theory in the Pacific, the Pacific in Theory: Archaeological Perspectives*, ed. T. Thomas, London: Routledge, 200–16.

Flexner, J. L., S. Bedford, & F. Valentin (2019). Who Was Polynesian? Who Was Melanesian? Hybridity and Ethnogenesis in the South Vanuatu Outliers. *Journal of Social Archaeology*, 19(3), 403–26.

Flexner, J. L., S. Bedford, F. Valentin, R. Shing, T. Kuautonga, & W. Zinger (2018a). Preliminary Results of the South Vanuatu Archaeological Survey: Cultural Landscapes, Excavation, and Radiocarbon Dating. *Asian Perspectives*, 57(2), 244–66.

Flexner, J. L. & M. Leclerc (2019). Complexities and Diversity in Archaeologies of Island Melanesia, in *Archaeologies of Island Melanesia: Current Approaches to Landscapes, Exchange, and Practice*, eds. M. Leclerc & J. L. Flexner, Canberra: Australian National University Press, 1–5.

Flexner, J. L., L. Lindstrom, F. R. Hickey, & J. Kapere (2018b). Kaio, Kapwier, Nepek, and Nuk: Human and Non-Human Agency, and 'Conservation' on Tanna, Vanuatu, in *Cultural and Spiritual Significance of Nature in Protected Areas: Governance, Management and Policy*, eds. B. Verschuuren & S. Brown, London: Routledge, 253–65.

Flexner, J. L., M. Spriggs, S. Bedford, & M. Abong (2016). Beginning Historical Archaeology in Vanuatu: Recent Projects on the Archaeology of Spanish, French, and Anglophone Colonialism, in *Archaeologies of Early Modern Spanish Colonialism*, eds. S. Montón-Subías, M. Cruz Berrocal, & A. Ruiz Martinez, New York: Springer, 205–27.

Flexner, J. L., E. Willie, A. Z. Lorey, H. Alderson, R. Williams, & S. Ieru (2016). Iarisi's Domain: Historical Archaeology of a Melanesian Village, Tanna Island, Vanuatu. *Journal of Island and Coastal Archaeology*, 11(1), 26–49.

Fornander, A. (1917). *Collection of Hawaiian Antiquities and Folk-Lore*, Honolulu, HI: B. P. Bishop Museum.

Garanger, J. (1972). *Archéologie des Nouvelles Hébrides*, Paris: Musée de l'Homme.

Garanger, J., (1996). Tongoa, Mangaasi and Retoka – History of a Prehistory, in *Arts of Vanuatu*, eds. J. Bonnemaison, K. Huffman, C. Kaufmann, & D. Tryon, Honolulu, HI: University of Hawaii Press, 66–73.

Gibbs, M. (2011). Beyond the New World: Exploring the Failed Spanish Colonies of the Solomon Islands, in *Historical Archaeology and the Importance of Material Things II*, eds. J. M. Schablitsky & M. Leone, Rockville, MD: The Society for Historical Archaeology, 143–66.

Glover, H. J., T. N. Ladefoged, and E. E. Cochrane (2020). Costly Signalling and the Distribution of Monumental Mounds in Savai'i and 'Upolu, Sāmoa. *Archaeology in Oceania*, 55, 141–152.

Golson, J., T. Denham, P. Hughes, P. Swadling, & J. Muke (eds.) (2017). *Ten Thousand Years of Cultivation at Kuk Swamp in the Highlands of Papua New Guinea*, Canberra: Australian National University Press.

Gongora, J., N. J. Rawlence, V. A. Mobegi, H. Jianlin, J. A. Alcalde, J. T. Matus, O. Hanotte, C. Moran, J. J. Austin, S. Ulm, A. Anderson, G. Larson, & A. Cooper (2008). Reply to Storey *et al.*: More DNA and Dating Studies Needed for Ancient El Arenal-1 Chickens. *Proceedings of the National Academy of Sciences*, 105(48), E100.

Gonzalez, S. L., I. Kretzler, & B. Edwards (2018). Imagining Indigenous and Archaeological Futures: Building Capacity with the Federated Tribes of Grande Ronde. *Archaeologies*, 14(1), 85–114.

Gosden, C. (2004). *Archaeology and Colonialism: Cultural Contact from 5000 BC to the Present*, Cambridge: Cambridge University Press.

Gosden, C. (2010). When Humans Arrived in the New Guinea Highlands. *Science*, 330, 41–2.

Graves, M. (1986). Organization and Differentiation within Late Prehistoric Ranked Social Units, Mariana Islands, Western Pacific. *Journal of Field Archaeology*, 13, 139–54.

Gray, W. (1892). *Notes on the Tannese*, Hobart: Australian Association for the Advancement of Science.

Gray, W. (1894). Four Aniwan Songs. *Journal of the Polynesian Society*, 3(2), 93–7.

Green, R. C. (1973). The Conquest of the Conquistadors. *World Archaeology*, 5 (1), 14–31.

Green, R. C. (1991). Near and Remote Oceania: Disestablishing 'Melanesia' in Culture History, in *Man and a Half: Essays in Pacific Anthropology and Ethnobiology in Honour of Ralph Bulmer*, ed. A. Pawley, Auckland: The Polynesian Society, 481–592.

Green, R. C. and J. Davidson (eds.) (1974). *Archaeology in Western Samoa*, Auckland: Auckland Institute and Museum.

Greenhill, S. J. (2015). TransNewGuinea.org: An Online Database of New Guinea Languages. *PLoS One.* DOI: https://doi.org/10.1371/journal .pone.0141563.

Guiart, J. (1982). A Polynesian Myth and the Invention of Melanesia. *Journal of the Polynesian Society*, 91(1), 139–44.

Guiart, J. (2013). *Cultures on the Edge: Caught Unwittingly between the White Man's Concepts of Polynesia Opposed to Melanesia, From Efate to Epi, Central Vanuatu*, Pape'ete: Te Pito o te Fenua.

Haddon, A. C. & J. Hornell (1938). *Canoes of Oceania*, Honolulu, HI: B. P. Bishop Museum Press.

Hather, J. and P. V. Kirch (1991). Prehistoric Sweet Potato (*Ipomoea batatas*) from Mangaia Island, Central Polynesia. *Antiquity*, 65, 887–93.

Hau'ofa, E. (1993). Our Sea of Islands, in *A New Oceania: Rediscovering Our Sea of Islands*, eds. V. Naidu, E. Wadell, & E. Hau'ofa, Suva: University of the South Pacific, 2–16.

Heyerdahl, T. (1952). *American Indians in the Pacific: The Theory behind the Kon-Tiki Expedition*, London: Allen and Unwin.

Hicks, D. (2013). Characterizing the World Archaeology Collections of the Pitt Rivers Museum, in *World Archaeology at the Pitt Rivers Museum: A Characterization*, eds. D. Hicks & A. Stevenson, Oxford: Archaeopress, 1–15.

Holdaway, R. N., M. E. Allentoft, C. Jacomb, C. L. Oskam, N. R. Beavan, & M. Bunce (2014). An Extremely Low-Density Human Population Exterminated New Zealand Moa. *Nature Communications*, 5(5436). DOI: https://doi.org/10.1038/ncomms6436.

Holmes, C. & N. Standen (2018). Introduction: Towards a Global Middle Ages. *Past and Present*, 238 (supplement 13), xii–xxi.

Horsburgh, A. & M. D. McCoy (2017). Dispersal, Isolation, and Interaction in the Islands of Polynesia: A Critical Review of Archaeological and Genetic Evidence. *Diversity*, 9(37), 1–21.

Howe, K. R. (ed.) (2006). *Vaka Moana: Voyages of the Ancestors*, Honolulu, HI: University of Hawaii Press.

Huffman, K. (1996). The 'Decorated Cloth' from the 'Island of Good Yams': Barkcloth in Vanuatu, with Special Reference to Erromango, in *Arts of Vanuatu*, eds. J. Bonnemaison, K. Huffman, C. Kaufmann, & D. Tryon, Honolulu, HI: University of Hawaii Press, 129–40.

Humphreys, C. B. (1926). *The Southern New Hebrides: An Ethnological Record*, Cambridge: Cambridge University Press.

Hunt, T. L. & C. P. Lipo (2009). Ecological Catastrophe, Collapse, and the Myth of 'Ecocide' on Rapa Nui (Easter Island), in *Questioning Collapse: Human*

Resilience, Ecological Vulnerability, and the Aftermath of Empire, eds.
P. A. McAnany & N. Yoffee, Cambridge: Cambridge University Press,
21–44.

Ioannidis, A. G., J. Blanco-Portillo, K. Sandoval, E. Hagelberg, J. F.
Miquel-Poblete, J. V. Moreno-Mayar, J. E. Rodríguez-Rodríguez,
C. D. Quinto-Cortés, K. Auckland, T. Parks, K. Robson, A. V. S.
Hill, M. C. Avila-Arcos, A. Sockell, J. R. Homburger, G. L. Wojcik,
K. C. Barnes, L. Herrera, S. Berríos, M. Acuña, E. Llop, C. Eng,
S. Huntsman, E. G. Burchard, C. R. Gignoux, L. Cifuentes, R. A.
Verdugo, M. Moraga, A. J. Mentzer, C. D. Bustamante, & A. Moreno-
Estrada (2020). Native American Gene Flow into Polynesia Predating
Easter Island Settlement. *Nature*, 583, 572–7.

Irwin, G. (1992). *The Prehistoric Exploration and Colonisation of the Pacific*,
Cambridge: Cambridge University Press.

Jacomb, C., R. N. Holdaway, M. E. Allentoft, M. Bunce, C. L. Oskam,
R. Walter, & E. Brooks (2014). High-Precision Dating and Ancient DNA
Profiling of Moa (Aves: Dinornithiformes) Eggshell Documents
a Complex Feature at Wairau Bar and Refines the Chronology of New
Zealand Settlement by Polynesians. *Journal of Archaeological Science*, 50,
24–30.

Johns, D. A., G. J. Irwin, and Y. K. Sung (2014). An Early Sophisticated East
Polynesian Voyaging Canoe Discovered on New Zealand's Coast.
Proceedings of the National Academy of Sciences, 111(41), 14728–33.

Jolly, M. (2009). The Sediment of Voyages: Remembering Quirós, Bougainville
and Cook in Vanuatu, in *Oceanic Encounters: Exchange, Desire, Violence*,
eds. M. Jolly, S. Tcherkézoff, & D. Tryon, Canberra: Australian National
University Press, 57–111.

Jones, T. L. & E. Klar (2005). Diffusionism Reconsidered: Linguistic and
Archaeological Evidence for Prehistoric Polynesian Contact with Southern
California. *American Antiquity*, 70, 457–84.

Jones, T. L. & E. Klar (2009). On Linguistics and Cascading Inventions:
A Comment on Arnold's Dismissal of a Polynesian Contact Event in
Southern California. *American Antiquity*, 74, 173–82.

Jones, T. L. & E. Klar (2012). A Land Visited: Reviewing the Case for
Polynesian Contact in Southern California, in *Contemporary Issues in
California Archaeology*, eds. T. L. Jones & J. E. Perry, Walnut Creek, CA:
Left Coast Press, 217–35.

Jones, T. L., A. A. Storey, E. Matisoo-Smith, & J. M. Ramirez-Aliaga (eds.)
(2011). *Polynesians in America: Pre-Columbian Contacts with the New
World*, Lanham, MD: Altamira Press.

Kamakau, S. M. (1976). *The Works of the People of Old: Na Hana a ka Poʻe Kahiko*, Honolulu, HI: B. P. Bishop Museum Press.

Kamakau, S. M. (1991). *Tales and Traditions of the People of Old: Nā Moʻolelo a ka Poʻe Kahiko*, Honolulu, HI: B. P. Bishop Museum Press.

Kawelu, K. L. & D. Pakele (2014). Community-Based Research: The Next Step in Hawaiian Archaeology. *Journal of Pacific Archaeology*, 5(2), 62–71.

Kealy, S., J. Louys, & S. O'Connor (2016). Islands Under the sea: A Review of Early Modern Human Dispersal Routes and Migration Hypotheses through Wallacea. *Journal of Island and Coastal Archaeology*, 11(3), 364–84.

Keller, J. D. & T. Kuautonga (2007). *Nokonofo Kitea, We Keep on Living this Way: Myths and Music of Futuna, Vanuatu*, Adelaide: Crawford House Publishing.

Kelloway, S. G., S. Craven, M. Pecha, W. R. Dickinson, M. Gibbs, T. Ferguson, & M. D. Glascock (2014). Sourcing Olive Jars Using U-Pb Ages of Detrital Zircons: A Study of 16th Century Olive Jars Recovered from the Solomon Islands. *Geoarchaeology*, 29, 47–60.

Kelloway, S. G., M. Gibbs, & S. Craven (2013). The Sherds of Conquistadors: A Petrological Study of Ceramics from Graciosa Bay and Pamua, Solomon Islands. *Archaeology in Oceania*, 48, 53–9.

Kelly, C. (ed.) (1966). *La Austrialia del Espíritu Santo: The Journal of Fray Martín de Munilla O.F.M. and Other Documents Relating to the Voyage of Pedro Fernández de Quirós to the South Sea (1605–1606) and the Franciscan Missionary Plan (1617–1627)*, Cambridge: The Hakluyt Society.

Kirch, P. V. (1984). The Polynesian Outliers: Continuity, Change and Replacement. *Journal of Pacific History*, 19(4), 224–38.

Kirch, P. V. (1988). *Niuatoputapu: The Prehistory of a Polynesian Chiefdom*, Seattle, WA: University of Washington Press.

Kirch, P. V. (1997a). Microcosmic Histories: Island Perspectives on 'Global' Change. *American Anthropologist*, 99(1), 30–42.

Kirch, P. V. (1997b). *The Lapita Peoples: Ancestors of the Oceanic World*, Oxford: Blackwell.

Kirch, P. V. (2004). Temple Sites in Kahikinui, Maui: Their Orientations Decoded. *Antiquity*, 78, 102–14.

Kirch, P. V. (2007). Hawaii as a Model System for Human Ecodynamics. *American Anthropologist*, 109(1), 8–26.

Kirch, P. V. (2010a). *How Chiefs Became Kings: Divine Kingship and the Rise of Archaic States in Ancient Hawaii*, Berkeley, CA: University of California Press.

Kirch, P. V. (2010b). Peopling of the Pacific: A Holistic Anthropological Perspective. *Annual Review of Anthropology*, 39, 131–48.

Kirch, P. V. (ed.) (2011). *Roots of Conflict: Soils, Agriculture, and Sociopolitical Complexity in Ancient Hawai'i*, Santa Fe, NM: School for Advanced Research Press.

Kirch, P. V. (2017). *On the Road of the Winds: An Archaeological History of the Pacific Islands before European Contact*, Berkeley, CA: University of California Press.

Kirch, P. V. (2018). Voices on the Wind, Traces in the Earth: Integrating Oral Narrative and Archaeology in Polynesian History. *Journal of the Polynesian Society*, 127(3), 275–306.

Kirch, P. V. (2021). Controlled Comparison and the Phylogenetic Model in Polynesian Culture History, in *Theory in the Pacific, the Pacific in Theory: Archaeological Perspectives*, ed. T. Thomas, London: Routledge, 79–101.

Kirch, P. V. & R. C. Green (2001). *Hawaiki, Ancestral Polynesia: An Essay in Historical Anthropology*, Cambridge: Cambridge University Press.

Kirch, P. V. & M. Kelly (1975). *Prehistory and Ecology of a Windward Hawaiian Valley: Halawa Valley, Molokai*, Honolulu, HI: B. P. Bishop Museum Press.

Kirch, P. V. & M. D. McCoy (2007). Reconfiguring the Hawaiian Cultural Sequence: Results of Re-Dating the Hālawa Dune Site (MO-A1-3), Moloka'i Island. *Journal of the Polynesian Society*, 116(4), 385–406.

Kirch, P. V., S. Millerstrom, S. Jones, & M. D. McCoy (2010). Dwelling among the Gods: A Late Pre-Contact Priest's House in Kahikinui, Maui, Hawaiian Islands. *Journal of Pacific Archaeology*, 1(2), 145–60.

Kirch, P. V., G. Molle, C. Nickelsen, P. Mills, E. Dotte-Sarout, J. Swift, A. Wolfe, & M. Horrocks (2015). Human Ecodynamics in the Mangareva Islands: A Stratified Sequence from Nenega-Iti Rock Shelter (Site AGA-3, Agakauitai Island). *Archaeology in Oceania*, 50(1), 23–42.

Kirch, P. V., G. Molle, E. M. Niespolo, & W. D. Sharp. (2021). Coordinated ^{14}C and [230]Th dating of Kitchen Cave Rockshelter, Gambier (Mangareva) Islands, French Polynesia: Comparing [230]Th Coral Dates with Bayesian Model Ages. *Journal of Archaeological Science: Reports*. DOI: https://doi.org/10.1016/j.jasrep.2020.102724

Kirch, P. V. & S. J. O'Day (2003). New Archaeological Insights into Food and Status: A Case Study from Pre-Contact Hawaii. *World Archaeology*, 34(3), 484–97.

Kirch, P. V. & P. H. Rosendahl (1973). Archaeological Investigations of Anuta, in *Anuta: A Polynesian Outlier in the Solomon Islands*, eds. D. E. Yen & J. Gordon, Honolulu, HI: B. P. Bishop Museum Press, 25–108.

Kirch, P. V. & C. Ruggles (2019). *Heiau, 'Āina, Lani: The Hawaiian Temple System in Ancient Kahikinui and Kaupō, Maui*, Honolulu, HI: University of Hawaii Press.

Kirch, P. V. & J. Swift (2017). New AMS Radiocarbon Dates and Re-Evaluation of Cultural Sequence of Tikopia, Southeast Solomon Islands. *Journal of the Polynesian Society*, 126(3), 313–36.

Kirch, P. V. & D. E. Yen (1982). *Tikopia: The Prehistory and Ecology of a Polynesian Outlier*, Honolulu, HI: B. P. Bishop Museum Press.

Kolb, M. J. (2006). The Origins of Monumental Architecture in Ancient Hawai'i. *Current Anthropology*, 47(4), 657–65.

Kusimba, C. (forthcoming). *Swahili Worlds in Globalism*. Cambridge: Cambridge University Press Elements Series in the Global Middle Ages.

Kuykendall, R. S. (1965). *The Hawaiian Kingdom, Vol. 1: 1778–1854 Foundation and Transformation*, Honolulu, HI: University of Hawaii Press.

Ladefoged, T. N., A. Flaws, & C. M. Stevenson (2013). The Distribution of Rock Gardens on Rapa Nui (Easter Island) as Determined from Satellite Imagery. *Journal of Archaeological Science*, 40, 1203–12.

Ladefoged, T. N. & M. Graves (2006). The Formation of Hawaiian Territories, in *Archaeology of Oceania: Australia and the Pacific Islands*, ed. I. Lilley, Oxford: Blackwell, 259–83.

Ladefoged, T. N., M. W. Graves, & M. D. McCoy (2003). Archaeological Evidence for Agricultural Development in Kohala, Island of Hawaii. *Journal of Archaeological Science*, 30, 923–40.

Ladefoged, T. N., P. V. Kirch, S. M. Gon, O. A. Chadwick, A. S. Hartshorn, & P. M. Vitousek (2009). Opportunities and Constraints for Intensive Agriculture in the Hawaiian Archipelago Prior to European Contact. *Journal of Archaeological Science*, 36, 2374–83.

Ladefoged, T. N., M. D. McCoy, G. P. Asner, P. V. Kirch, C. P. Poulsen, O. A. Chadwick, & P. M. Vitousek (2011). Agricultural Potential and Actualized Development in Hawai'i: An Airborne LiDAR Survey of the Leeward Kohala Field System (Hawai'i Island). *Journal of Archaeological Science*, 38, 3605–19.

Leach, F. & J. Davidson (2008). *The Archaeology of Taumako: A Polynesian Outlier in the Eastern Solomon Islands*, Auckland: *New Zealand Journal of Archaeology* Special Publication.

Leclerc, M. & J. L. Flexner (eds.) (2019). *Archaeologies of Island Melanesia: Current Approaches to Lanscapes, Exchange, and Practice*, Canberra: Australian National University Press.

Levison, M., R. G. Ward, & J. W. Webb. (1972). The Settlement of Polynesia: A Report on a Computer Simulation. *Archaeology and Physical Anthropology in Oceania*, 7(3), 234–45.

Lightfoot, K. G. (1995). Culture Contact Studies: Redefining the Relationship between Prehistoric and Historical Archaeology. *American Antiquity*, 60(2), 199–217.

Lindstrom, L. (2004). History, Folklore, Traditional and Current Uses of Kava, in *Kava: From Ethnology to Pharmacology*, ed. Y. N. Singh, London: Taylor and Francis, 10–28.

Lindstrom, L. (2011). Naming and Memory on Tanna, Vanuatu, in *Changing Contexts, Shifting Meanings: Transformations of Cultural Traditions in Oceania*, ed. E. Hermann, Honolulu, HI: University of Hawaii Press, 141–56.

Luque, M. & C. Mondragón (2005). Faith, Fidelity, and Fantasy: Don Pedro Fernández de Quirós and the 'Foundation, Government, and Sustenance' of La Nueba Hierusalem in 1606. *Journal of Pacific History*, 40(2), 133–48.

Lydon, J. (2006). Pacific Encounters, or Beyond the Islands of History, in *Historical Archaeology*, eds. M. Hall & S. W. Silliman, Oxford: Blackwell, 293–312.

Lynch, J. (1996). Kava-Drinking in Southern Vanuatu: Melanesian Drinkers, Polynesian Roots. *Journal of the Polynesian Society*, 105(1), 27–40.

MacKay, A. (1977). *Spain in the Middle Ages: From Frontier to Empire, 1000–1500*, London: MacMillan.

Malo, D. (1951). *Hawaiian Antiquities: Mo'olelo Hawai'i*, Honolulu, HI: B. P. Bishop Museum Press.

Maor, E. (2004). *Venus in Transit*, Princeton, NJ: Princeton University Press.

Markham, C. (ed.) (1904). *The Voyages of Pedro Fernandez de Quiros, 1595 to 1606*, Cambridge: The Hakluyt Society.

Marshall, Y. (2021). Taking Indigenous Theory Seriously: *Whakapapa* and Chevron Pendants, in *Theory in the Pacific, the Pacific in Theory: Archaeological Perspectives*, ed. T. Thomas, London: Routledge, 299–328.

Martinsson-Wallin, H. (2011). The Complexity of an Archaeological Site in Samoa: The Past in the Present, in *Pacific Island Heritage: Archaeology, Identity, and Community*, eds. J. Liston, G. Clark, & D. Alexander, Canberra: Australian National University Press, 101–14.

Martinsson-Wallin, H. (2014). Archaeological Investigations of Independent Samoa: *Tala eli* of Laupule Mound and Beyond, in *Monuments and People in the Pacific*, ed. H. Martinsson-Wallin & T. Thomas, Uppsala: Uppsala University Department of Archaeology and Ancient History, 245–72.

Martinsson-Wallin, H., P. Wallin, & G. Clark (2007). The Excavation of Pulemelei Site 2002–2004. *Archaeology in Oceania*, 42(1(supplement)), 41–59.

Matisoo-Smith, E. (2011). Human Biological Evidence for Polynesian Contacts with the Americas: Finding Maui on Mocha?, in *Polynesians in America: Pre-Columbian Contacts with the New World*, eds. T. L. Jones, A. A. Storey, E. Matisoo-Smith, & J. M. Ramirez-Aliaga, Lanham, MD: Altamira, 208–22.

Matisoo-Smith, E. & J. M. Ramirez (2010). Human Skeletal Evidence of Polynesian Presence in South America? Metric Analyses of Six Crania from Mocha Island, Chile. *Journal of Pacific Archaeology*, 1(1), 76–88.

McCoy, M. D. (2005). The Development of the Kalaupapa Field System, Moloka'i Island, Hawai'i. *Journal of the Polynesian Society*, 114, 339–58.

McCoy, M. D. (2014). The Significance of Religious Ritual in Ancient Hawai'i. *Journal of Pacific Archaeology*, 5(2), 72–80.

McCoy, M. D., H. A. Alderson, R. Hemi, H. Cheng, & R. L. Edwards (2016). Earliest Direct Evidence of Monument Building at the Archaeological Site of Nan Madol (Pohnpei, Micronesia) Identified Using 230Th/U Coral Dating and Geochemical Sourcing of Megalithic Architectural Stone. *Quarternary Research*, 86, 295–303.

McCoy, M. D., H. Alderson, & A. Thompson (2015). A New Archaeological Field Survey of the Site of Nan Madol, Pohnpei. *Rapa Nui Journal*, 29(1), 5–22.

McCoy, M. D. & J. Carpenter. (2014). Strategies for Obtaining Obsidian in Pre-European Contact Era New Zealand. *PLoS-One*, 9(1), 1–13.

McCoy, M. D., C. Cervera, M. A. Mulrooney, A. McAlister, & P. V. Kirch (2020). Obsidian and Volcanic Glass Artifact Evidence for Long-Distance Voyaging to the Polynesian Outlier Island of Tikopia. *Quarternary Research*. DOI: https://doi.org/10.1017/qua.2020.38.

McCoy, M. D. & M. C. Codlin (2017). The Influence of Religious Authority in Everyday Life: A Landscape-Scale Study of Domestic Architecture and Religious Law in Ancient Hawai'i. *World Archaeology*, 48(3), 411–30.

McCoy, M. D. & M. Graves (2010). The Role of Agricultural Innovation in Pacific Islands: A Case Study from Hawai'i Island. *World Archaeology*, 42 (1), 90–107.

McCoy, M. D., T. N. Ladefoged, M. Codlin, & D. Sutton (2014). Does Carneiro's Circumscription Theory Help Us Understand Maori History? An Analysis of the Obsidian Assemblage from Pouerua Pa, New Zealand (Aotearoa). *Journal of Archaeological Science*, 42(1), 467–75.

Mead, H. M. (2003). *Tikanga Māori: Living by Māori Values*, Wellington: Huia Publishers.

Melander, V. (2019). David's Weapon of Mass Destruction: The Reception of Thor Heyerdahl's 'Kon-Tiki Theory'. *Bulletin of the History of Archaeology*, 29(1), 1–11.

Mulrooney, M. A., S. H. Bickler, M. S. Allen, & T. N. Ladefoged (2011). Letter: High-Precision Dating of Colonization and Settlement in East Polynesia. *Proceedings of the National Academy of Sciences*, 108(23), 192–4.

Naupa, A. (ed.) (2011). *Nompi en Ovoteme Erromango (Kastom and Culture of Erromango)*, Port Vila: Erromango Cultural Association.

Obeyesekere, G. (1992). *The Apotheosis of Captain Cook: European Mythmaking in the Pacific*, Princeton, NJ: Princeton University Press.

O'Regan, G. (2016). He ana, he whakairo: Examining Māori Belief of Place Through the Archaeological Context of Rock Art. Unpublished PhD thesis, University of Auckland.

Parke, A. (2014). *Degei's Descendants: Spirits, Place, and People in Pre-Cession Fiji*, Canberra: Australian National University Press.

Pawley, A. (2009). The Role of the Solomon Islands in the First Settlement of Remote Oceania: Bringing Linguistic Evidence to an Archaeological Debate, in *Austronesian Historical Linguistics and Culture History: A Festschrift for Robert Blust*, eds. A. Adelaar & A. Pawley, Canberra: RSPAS, The Australian National University, 515–40.

Phillips, C. (2000). Post-Contact Landscapes of Change in Hauraki, New Zealand, in *The Archaeology of Difference: Negotiating Cross-Cultural Engagements in Oceania*, eds. R. Torrence & A. Clarke, London: Routledge, 79–104.

Pomeranz, K. (2009). Calamities without Collapse: Environment, Economy, and Society in China, ca. 1800–1914, in *Questioning Collapse: Human Resilience, Ecological Vulnerability, and the Aftermath of Empire*, eds. P. A. McAnany & N. Yoffee, Cambridge: Cambridge University Press, 71–112.

Poulsen, J. I. (1972). Outlier Archaeology: Bellona. A Preliminary Report on Field Work and Radiocarbon Dates: Part I. – Archaeology. *Archaeology and Physical Anthropology in Oceania*, 7(3), 184–205.

Price, N. (2018). Distant Vikings: A Manifesto. *Acta Archaeologica*, 89, 113–32.

Price, N. & J. Ljungkvist (2018). Polynesians of the Atlantic? Precedents, Potentials, and Pitfalls in Oceanic Analogies of the Vikings. *Danish Journal of Archaeology*, 7(2), 133–8.

Rainbird, P. (2004). *The Archaeology of Micronesia*, Cambridge: Cambridge University Press.

Ravn, M. (2018). Roads to Complexity: Hawaiians and Vikings Compared. *Danish Journal of Archaeology*, 7(2), 119–32.

Rieth, T. M., T. L. Hunt, C. P. Lipo, & J. M. Wilmshurst (2011). The 13th Century Polynesian Colonization of Hawai'i Island. *Journal of Archaeological Science*, 38, 2740–9.

Rigby, N., P. van der Merwe, & G. Williams (2005). *Pioneers of the Pacific: Voyages of Exploration, 1787–1810*, London: National Maritime Museum.

Robin, C., M. Monzier, & J.-P. Eissen (1994). Formation of the Mid-Fifteenth Century Kuwae Caldera (Vanuatu) by an Initial Hydroclastic and Subsequent Ignimbritic Eruption. *Bulletin of Volcanology*, 56, 170–83.

Roullier, C., L. Benoit, D. McKey, & V. Lebot (2013). Historical Collections Reveal Patterns of Diffusion of Sweet Potato in Oceania Obscured by Modern Plant Movements and Recombination. *Proceedings of the National Academy of Sciences*, 110(6), 2205–10.

Sahlins, M. (1963). Poor Man, Rich Man, Big-Man, Chief: Political Types in Melanesia and Polynesia. *Comparative Studies in Society and History*, 5(3), 285–303.

Sahlins, M. (1985). *Islands of History*, Chicago, IL: The University of Chicago Press.

Sahlins, M. (1992). *Anahulu: The Anthropology of History in the Kingdom of Hawai'i. Volume 1, Historical Ethnography*, Chicago, IL: University of Chicago Press.

Sahlins, M. (1995). *How 'Natives' Think, About Captain Cook, For Example*, Chicago, IL: The University of Chicago Press.

Salmond, A. (1991). *Two Worlds: First Meetings between Maori and Europeans 1642–1772*, Honolulu, IL: University of Hawaii Press.

Salmond, A. (2003). *The Trial of the Cannibal Dog: The Remarkable Story of Captain Cook's Encounters in the South Seas*, New Haven, CT: Yale University Press.

Salmond, A. (2009). *Aphrodite's Island: The European Discovery of Tahiti*, Berkeley, CA: University of California Press.

Salmond, A. (2011). *Bligh: William Bligh in the South Seas*, Auckland: Viking-Penguin.

Sand, C. (1996). Structural Remains as Markers of Complex Societies in Southern Melanesia during Prehistory: The Case of the Monumental Forts of Mare Island (New Caledonia). *Bulletin of the Indo-Pacific Prehistory Association*, 15(2), 37–44.

Sand, C. (1998). Recent Archaeological Research in the Loyalty Islands of New Caledonia. *Asian Perspectives*, 37(2), 194–223.

Sand, C. (2002). Melanesian Tribes vs. Polynesian Chiefdoms: Recent Archaeological Assessment of a Classic Model of Sociopolitical Types in Oceania. *Asian Perspectives*, 41(2), 284–96.

Sand, C., J. Bole, & A. Ouetcho (2003). Prehistory and its Perception in a Melanesian Archipelago: the New Caledonia Example. *Antiquity*, 77 (297), 505–19.

Schlunke, K. (2007). Historicising Whiteness: Captain Cook Possesses Australia, in *Historicising Whiteness: Transnational Perspectives on the Construction of an Identity*, eds. L. Boucher, J. Carey, & K. Ellinghaus, Melbourne: RMIT Publishing, 41–50.

Schmidt, P. R. & I. Pikirayi (2018). Will Historical Archaeology Escape its Western Prejudices to Become Relevant to Africa? *Archaeologies*, 14(3), 443–71.

Scott, J. C. (2009). *The Art of Not Being Governed: An Anarchist History of Upland Southeast Asia*, New Haven, CT: Yale University Press.

Sear, D. A., M. S. Allen, J. D. Hassalla, A. E. Maloney, P. G. Langdona, A. E. Morrison, A. C. G. Hendersone, H. Mackaye, I. W. Croudace, C. Clarke, J. P. Sachsc, G. Macdonald, R. C. Chiverrellg, M. J. Lengh, L. M. Cisneros-Dozalj, & T. Fonvillea (2020). Human Settlement of East Polynesia Earlier, Incremental, and Coincident with Prolonged South Pacific Drought. *Proceedings of the National Academy of Sciences*. DOI: https://doi.org/10.1073/pnas.1920975117.

Sheehan, C. (2008). Strangers and Servants of the Company: The United East India Company and the Dutch Voyages to Australia, in *Strangers on the Shore: Early Coastal Contacts in Australia*, eds. P. Veth, P. Sutton, & M. Neale, Canberra: National Museum of Australia, 6–34.

Sheppard, P. (2019). Four Hundred Years of Niche Construction in the Western Solomon Islands, in *Archaeologies of Island Melanesia: Current Approaches to Landscapes, Exchange, and Practice*, eds. M. Leclerc & J. L. Flexner, Canberra: Australian National University Press, 117–34.

Sherwood, S. C., J. A. Van Tilburg, C. R. Barrier, M. Horrocks, R. K. Dunn, & J. M. Ramirez-Aliaga (2019). New Excavations in Easter Island's Statue Quarry: Soil Fertility, Site Formation and Chronology. *Journal of Archaeological Science*. DOI: https://doi.org/10.1016/j.jas.2019.104994.

Sinoto, Y. H. (1979). Excavations in Huahine, French Polynesia. *Pacific Studies*, 3, 1–40.

Sinoto, Y. H. & McCoy, P. C. (1975). Report on the Preliminary Excavation of an Early Habitation Site on Huahine, Society Islands. *Journal de la Société des Océanistes*, 47, 143–86.

Smith, A. (2007). Building Capacity in Pacific Island Heritage Management: Lessons from Those Who Know Best. *Archaeologies*, 3(3), 335–52.

Smith, I. W. G. (2005). Retreat and Resilience: Fur Seals and Human Settlement in New Zealand, in *The Exploitation and Cultural Importance of Sea Mammals*, ed. G. Monks, Oxford: Oxbow Books, 6–18.

Smith, I. W. G. (2014). Oceania: Historical Archaeology, in *Encyclopedia of Global Archaeology*, ed. C. Smith, New York: Springer. DOI: https://doi.org /10.1007/978-1-4419-0465-2.

Sobel, D. (1995). *Longitude: The True Story of a Lone Genius who Solved the Greatest Scientific Problem of His Time*, New York: Penguin.

Spate, O. H. (2004 [1979]). *The Spanish Lake*, Canberra: Australian National University Press.

Spriggs, M. (1981). Vegetable Kingdoms: Taro Irrigation and Pacific Prehistory. Unpublished PhD thesis, Australian National University.

Spriggs, M. (1986). Landscape, Land Use, and Political Transformation in Southern Melanesia, in *Island Societies: Archaeological Approaches to Evolution and Transformation*, ed. P. V. Kirch, Cambridge: University of Cambridge Press, 6–19.

Spriggs, M. (1992). 'Auwai, Kanawai and Waiwai: Irrigation in Kawailoa-Uka, in *Anahulu: The Anthropology of History in the Kingdom of Hawaii*, ed. P. V. Kirch, Chicago, IL: University of Chicago Press, 118–64.

Spriggs, M. (1997). *The Island Melanesians*, Oxford: Blackwell.

Spriggs, M. (2007). Population in a Vegetable Kingdom: Aneityum Island (Vanuatu) at European Contact in 1830, in *The Growth and Collapse of Pacific Island Societies: Archaeological and Demographic Perspectives*, eds. P. V. Kirch & J.-L. Rallu, Honolulu, HI: University of Hawaii Press, 278–305.

Spriggs, M. (2008). Ethnographic Parallels and the Denial of History. *World Archaeology*, 40(4), 538–52.

Spriggs, M. (2016). Thoughts of a Comparativist on Past Colonisation, Maritime Interaction and Cultural Integration, in *Comparative Perspectives on Past Colonisation, Maritime Interaction and Cultural Integration*, eds. L. Melheim, H. Glørstad, & Z. L. Glørstad, Sheffield: Equinox, 271–80.

Stevenson, C. M., T. N. Ladefoged, & S. Haoa (2002). Productive Strategies in an Uncertain Environment. *Rapa Nui Journal*, 16(1), : :17–22.

Storey, A. A., D. Quiroz, N. R. Beavan, & E. Matisoo-Smith (2013). Polynesian Chickens in the New World: A Detailed Application of a Commensal Approach. *Archaeology in Oceania*, 48(2), 101–19.

Storey, A. A., D. Quiroz, J. M. Ramirez-Aliaga, N. R. Beavan-Athfield, D. Addison, R. Walter, T. L. Hunt, J. S. Athens, L. Huynen, & E. Matisoo-Smith (2008). Pre-Columbian Chickens, Dates, Isotopes, and mtDNA. *Proceedings of the National Academy of Sciences*, 105(48), E99.

Storey, A. A., J. M. Ramirez-Aliaga, D. Quiroz, D. V. Burley, D. Addison, R. Walter, A. Anderson, T. L. Hunt, J. S. Athens, L. Huynen, & E. Matisoo-Smith (2007). Radiocarbon and DNA Evidence for a Pre-Columbian

Introduction of Polynesian Chickens to Chile. *Proceedings of the National Academy of Sciences*, 104(25), 10335–9.

Strathern, M. (1990). *The Gender of the Gift: Problems with Women and Problems with Society in Melanesia*, Berkeley, CA: University of California Press.

Summers, C. (1971). *Molokai: A Site Survey*, Honolulu, HI: B. P. Bishop Museum Press.

Swift, J., P. Roberts, N. Boivin, & P. V. Kirch (2018). Restructuring of Nutrient Flows in Island Ecosystems Following Human Colonization Evidenced by Isotopic Analysis of Commensal Rats. *Proceedings of the National Academy of Sciences*, 115(25), 6392–7.

Taonui, R. (2015). Whakapapa – Genealogy, in *Te Ara – the Encyclopedia of New Zealand*. https://teara.govt.nz/en/whakapapa-genealogy (accessed 13 July 2020).

Thomas, T. (2019). Axes of Entanglement in the New Georgia Group, Solomon Islands, in *Archaeologies of Island Melanesia: Current Approaches to Landscapes, Exchange, and Practice*, eds. M. Leclerc & J. L. Flexner, Canberra: Australian National University Press, 103–16.

UNESCO (2019). *Operational Guidelines for the Implementation of the World Heritage Convention*, Paris: UNESCO World Heritage Centre.

Van Tilburg, J. A. (1994). *Easter Island: Archaeology, Ecology, and Culture*, Washington, DC: Smithsonian Institution Press.

Vitousek, P. M., 2018. *Nutrient Cycling and Limitation: Hawaii as a Model System*, Princeton, NJ: Princeton University Press.

Vitousek, P. M., T. N. Ladefoged, A. S. Hartshorn, P. V. Kirch, M. Graves, S. Hotchkiss, S. Tuljapurkar, & O. A. Chadwick (2004). Soils, Agriculture, and Society in Precontact Hawai'i. *Science*, 304, 1665–9.

Von Haast, J. (1872). Moas and Moa Hunters. *Transactions of the New Zealand Institute*, 4, 66–107.

Walker, R. (1990). *Ka Whawhai Tonu Matou: Struggle Without End*, Auckland: Penguin Books.

Wallerstein, I. (1974). *The Modern World-System: Capitalist Agriculture and the Origins of the European World-Economy in the Sixteenth Century*, New York: Academic Press.

Walter, R., H. Buckley, C. Jacomb, & E. Matisoo-Smith. (2017). Mass Migration and the Polynesian Settlement of New Zealand. *Journal of World Prehistory*, 30, 351–76.

Walter, R. & P. Sheppard (2017). *Archaeology of the Solomon Islands*, Honolulu, HI: University of Hawaii Press.

Walter, R., T. Thomas, & P. J. Sheppard (2004). Cult Assemblages and Ritual Practice in Roviana Lagoon, Solomon Islands. *World Archaeology*, 36(1), 142–57.

Wehi, P. M. Wehi, N. J. Scott, J. Beckwith, R. Pryor Rodgers, T. Gillies, V. Van Uitregt, & K. Watene (2021). A Short Scan of Māori Journeys to Antarctica. *Journal of the Royal Society of New Zealand*. DOI: https://doi.org/10.1080/03036758.2021.1917633.

Weisler, M. I. (1994). The Settlement of Marginal Polynesia: New Evidence from Henderson Island. *Journal of Field Archaeology*, 21(1), 83–102.

Weisler, M. I. & P. V. Kirch (1985). The Structure of Settlement Space in a Polynesian Chiefdom: Kawela, Molokai, Hawaiian Islands. *New Zealand Journal of Archaeology*, 7, 129–58.

Williams, M. (2021). *Polynesia, 900–1600: An Overview of the History of Aotearoa, Rēkohu, and Rapa Nui*, Christchurch: Canterbury University Press.

Willie, E. (2019). A Melanesian View of Archaeology in Vanuatu, in *Archaeologies of Island Melanesia: Current Approaches to Landscapes, Exchange, and Practice*, eds. M. Leclerc & J. L. Flexner, Canberra: Australian National University Press, 211–14.

Wilmshurst, J. M., T. L. Hunt, C. P. Lipo, & A. Anderson (2011). High-Precision Radiocarbon Dating Shows Recent and Rapid Initial Human Colonization of East Polynesia. *Proceedings of the National Academy of Sciences*, 108(5), 1815–20.

Wilson, W. H. (2018). The Northern Outliers-East Polynesian Hypothesis Expanded. *Journal of the Polynesian Society*, 127(4), 389–423.

Wolf, E. R. (1982). *Europe and the People Without History*, Berkeley, CA: University of California Press.

Wozniak, J. A. (1999). Prehistoric Horticultural Practices on Easter Island: Lithic Mulched Gardens and Field Systems. *Rapa Nui Journal*, 13, 95–9.

Yen, D. E. (1974). *The Sweet Potato and Oceania: An Essay in Ethnobotany*, Honolulu, HI: B. P. Bishop Museum Press.

Zinger, W., F. Valentin, J. L. Flexner, S. Bedford, F. Détroit, & D. Grimaud-Hervé. (2020). How to Explain Polynesian Outliers' Heterogeneity?, in *Networks and Monumentality in the Pacific*, eds. A. Hermann, F. Valentin, C. Sand, & É. Nolet, Oxford: Archaeopress, 62–77.

Acknowledgements

I would like to thank Geraldine Heng for the invitation to contribute a volume on Oceania for the Cambridge Elements series and Susan Noakes for moving the manuscript through the editorial process. My own fieldwork in Oceania since 2006 has been supported by the University of California, Berkeley where I was a PhD student; Washington and Lee University; the Australian National University; and the University of Sydney. In the latter two cases I have received external funding from the Australian Research Council to support fieldwork and other analyses (DE130101703, DP160103578). I am extremely lucky to have a supportive and energetic group of colleagues working in the Pacific region. Some of the ideas in this book have emerged from long-standing conversations with Patrick Kirch, my PhD supervisor at Berkeley; Matthew Spriggs, a senior mentor when I was a postdoctoral researcher; Stuart Bedford, Frederique Valentin, Richard Shing, Edson Willie, and Iarowoi Philp, colleagues in Vanuatu research; and fellow Oceania scholars Mark McCoy, Mathieu Leclerc, Ben Shaw, Jenny Kahn, Jillian Swift, Guillaume Molle, Sandra Monton-Subias, Annie Clarke, Robin Torrence, Jude Philp, Peter White, Miranda Johnson, Leah Lui-Chivizhe, Helene Martinsson-Wallin, Tim Thomas, the late Ian Smith, the late Angela Middleton, and many others. My wife and dogs have my eternal thanks for putting up with my long trips to various Pacific Islands and collections of Islander things around the world. This book is dedicated to two high chiefs from Vanuatu who were mentors of mine, Jerry Taki and Jacob Kapere, both of whom passed to the realm of the ancestors far too soon. While many have helped me along the way, this Element is entirely my own work. Any errors and lacunae are my responsibility.

About the Author

James Flexner is Senior Lecturer in Historical Archaeology and Heritage at the University of Sydney. He is the author of *An Archaeology of Early Christianity in Vanuatu* (2016), and co-editor of *Archaeologies of Island Melanesia* (2019) and *Community-Led Research: Walking New Pathways Together* (2021). James is an archaeologist with extensive fieldwork experience in Oceania and Australia, including projects focusing on Molokai, South Vanuatu, Tasmania, and coastal Queensland. He has received multiple grants and fellowships from the Australian Research Council to support this research (DE130101703, DP160103578, LP170100048, FT210100244). James' research programme involves substantial collaborations with indigenous as well as settler communities.

Cambridge Elements ≡

The Global Middle Ages

Geraldine Heng

University of Texas at Austin

Geraldine Heng is Perceval Professor of English and Comparative Literature at the University of Texas, Austin. She is the author of *The Invention of Race in the European Middle Ages* (2018) and *England and the Jews: How Religion and Violence Created the First Racial State in the West* (2018), both published by Cambridge, as well as *Empire of Magic: Medieval Romance and the Politics of Cultural Fantasy* (2003, Columbia). She is the editor of *Teaching the Global Middle Ages* (2022, MLA), coedits the University of Pennsylvania Press series, RaceB4Race: Critical Studies of the Premodern, and is working on a new book, Early Globalisms: The Interconnected World, 500-1500 CE. Originally from Singapore, Heng is a Fellow of the Medieval Academy of America, a member of the Medievalists of Color, and Founder and Co-director, with Susan Noakes, of the Global Middle Ages Project: www.globalmiddleages.org

Susan Noakes

University of Minnesota Twin Cities

Susan Noakes is Professor and Chair of French and Italian at the University of Minnesota, Twin Cities. From 2002 to 2008 she was Director of the Center for Medieval Studies; she has also served as Director of Italian Studies, Director of the Center for Advanced Feminist Studies, and Associate Dean for Faculty in the College of Liberal Arts. Her publications include *The Comparative Perspective on Literature: Essays in Theory and Practice* (co-edited with Clayton Koelb, Cornell, 1988) and *Timely Reading: Between Exegesis and Interpretation* (Cornell, 1988), along with many articles and critical editions in several areas of French, Italian, and neo-Latin Studies. She is the Founder and Co-director, with Geraldine Heng, of the Global Middle Ages Project: www.globalmiddleages.org

About the Series

Elements in the Global Middle Ages is a series of concise studies that introduce researchers and instructors to an uncentered, interconnected world, c. 500–1500 CE. Individual Elements focus on the globe's geographic zones, its natural and built environments, its cultures, societies, arts, technologies, peoples, ecosystems, and lifeworlds.

Cambridge Elements ⹀

The Global Middle Ages

Elements in the Series

The Global Middle Ages: An Introduction
Geraldine Heng

The Market in Poetry in the Persian World
Shahzad Bashir

Oceania, 800-1800CE: A Millennium of Interactions in a Sea of Islands
James L. Flexner

A full series listing is available at: www.cambridge.org/EGMA

CPSIA information can be obtained
at www.ICGtesting.com
Printed in the USA
LVHW080304241221
707030LV00014B/1997